STOP what you're do~~ing and read~~ stop doing the things that are sucking your time, head space and creativity. Donna once again brings practical, fluff-free guidance to regain space and time to spend on what matters most.

— **Steph Clarke, facilitator, designer and podcaster** (*Steph's Business Bookshelf*)

Organisations have always asked 'how do we get the most done in the shortest amount of time?'. The question for us as individuals is, 'how can I best spend my own time?' Donna makes work work and in this brilliant addition to her productivity series, she tackles the relationship between work and time, and shows us how to get a refund of our most valuable commodity – time.

— **Matt Church author of *Rise Up: an evolution in leadership* and founder of Thought Leaders**

We all remember a great teacher. Holding attention. Caring to make important matters practical and bringing joy to life. Donna is such a teacher. She brings care, attention and practicality into her teaching and writing about time, every time. In her latest book *The 1-Day Refund*, Donna puts a powerful promise on the cover, that's not left hanging. It's great to know there's a bit of science behind the 85% that yields flow, Donna then delivers the ideas, tools and techniques to think differently about how we achieve this. How we govern time ourselves makes for a better leader in each of us.

The 1-Day Refund completes Donna's 'Trilogy on Time' — it's a great bookend to her teaching and writing on being effective with the time we have available and making life better for everyone.

— **Dr Richard Hodge, This Century Leadership and Governance, DrRichardHodge.com**

The productivity section of the self-help bookshelf has never been my cup of tea. The genre has always been so intensely focused on maximising our ability to produce stuff that it rarely seemed conducive to actually enjoying a full and balanced life.

For that reason, Donna McGeorge's contributions deserve to be a category unto themselves. *The 25 Minute Meeting* and *The First 2 Hours* are each a gift to those of us that want to unshackle ourselves from the busyness of the status quo and embrace a life of calm and control. In that vein, I think the book you hold in your hands might be Donna's coup-de-grace. The stand-out quote from the introduction is 'Instead of trading time for money, we need to trade energy for impact', which resonates down to my soul, and in true Donna McGeorge style the pages that follow describe and unpack a strategy for helping you achieve exactly that.

Since reading this book I'm trying a number of the experiments Donna suggests, with some very encouraging results. If you too deserve a day of your time back, I heartily endorse Donna and the ideas shared in this book.

— **Col Fink, speaker, author of** *Speakership* **and** *Tribe of Learning*, **head of programs at Thought Leaders**

Anyone who can give me back an extra day each week is a total genius! Thanks Donna.

— **Kieran Flanagan, speaker and author of** *Selfish, Scared & Stupid* **and** *Forever Skills*

THE
1 DAY
REFUND

IT'S ABOUT TIME

THE
1DAY
REFUND
TAKE BACK TIME
SPEND IT WISELY

DONNA
McGEORGE

WILEY

First published in 2022 by John Wiley & Sons Australia, Ltd
42 McDougall St, Milton Qld 4064
Office also in Melbourne

Typeset in Bembo Std 12/15pt

© John Wiley & Sons Australia, Ltd 2022

The moral rights of the author have been asserted

ISBN: 978-0-730-39820-2

A catalogue record for this book is available from the National Library of Australia

Cover design by Wiley
Cover and part opener image: © Ankudi/Getty Images
Internal illustrations by Donna McGeorge

Disclaimer

The material in this publication is of the nature of general comment only, and does not represent professional advice. It is not intended to provide specific guidance for particular circumstances and it should not be relied on as the basis for any decision to take action or not take action on any matter which it covers. Readers should obtain professional advice where appropriate, before making any such decision. To the maximum extent permitted by law, the author and publisher disclaim all responsibility and liability to any person, arising directly or indirectly from any person taking or not taking action based on the information in this publication.

SKY6835C75C-0ADD-4ED7-823C-F48D1F042AD5_032922

Contents

About the author   *ix*

Acknowledgements   *xi*

Introduction   *xiii*

How to use this book   *xvii*

Part I: Why we need to take back time   **1**

1   We're busy addicts   5

2   We need the capacity to adapt   17

3   We perform best with less   31

Part II: How to spend your time wisely   **39**

4   Thinking space   45

5   Breathing space   65

6   Living space   85

7   Working space   105

Final chapter bonus!   *129*

Your savings plan   *133*

Where to now?   *135*

Work with me   *139*

Sources   *141*

Index   *147*

About the author

Donna McGeorge makes work *work*.

She is passionate about enhancing the time we spend in the workplace (too much, for many of us) to ensure it is effective and productive, and enjoyable.

Donna has worked with managers and leaders throughout Australia and the Asia–Pacific for over 20 years. In 2020 she, like many of us, transitioned her work from live, in-person to online. She delivers productivity programs, keynotes and webinars globally across a mix of industries.

Her CV is as eclectic as her record collection (yes, classic vinyl). In addition to roles at Telstra, Qantas, Ernst & Young and Ansett, she has managed Theatre, Sports and Concert Tours for the UK-based travel company Keith Prowse and been the Asia–Pacific Organisational Development Manager for the Ford Motor Company in Shanghai.

Donna also shares her knowledge for good through appearances on *The Today Show*, radio interviews across Australia and writing articles for publications including *The Age*, *Boss Magazine*, *Smart Company*, *B&T Magazine* and *HRM*.

The 1-Day Refund is the third book in her 'It's About Time' productivity series. The other two are *The 25-Minute Meeting* and *The First 2 Hours*, published by John Wiley & Sons in 2018 and 2019 respectively.

She runs her business from her home in Hope Island, South East Queensland, a region known for its world-class beaches, but her most creative moments come while sipping tea on her balcony and gazing at the meandering waterways with her husband, Steve, and her dog, Prudence.

Donna believes that while workplaces are complex, they are not hard. More often than not it's getting the simple things right, consistently, that has the greatest impact.

She also knows that when we decide to be intentional, we can surprise ourselves with what we can achieve.

www.donnamcgeorge.com

Acknowledgements

In 2018 I published my first 'proper' book, *The 25-Minute Meeting*. It was a super-steep learning curve, and I couldn't have done it without the team who supported me. In 2019, just a year later, I published *The First 2 Hours* and, following the global pandemic, here I am in 2021, publishing my third book. Again, it has been a team effort.

Lucy Raymond, Chris Shorten, Renee Aurish and the team at Wiley—thank you for offering me the opportunity to turn two books into a series and working hard with me to get the title and message right for this one. You have opened up my work to the world and I'm forever grateful.

Kelly Irving—legend. We worked at a rocking pace for this one! I have come to rely heavily not only on your editing skill but on your intellect, your deep knowledge (no doubt from reading HEAPS of books) and your no-nonsense approach to writing great business books. Blessed to have you in my world.

Janine Garner—you loved my stuff so much you started sharing it far and wide before it was even fully developed in my head! Thank you for putting me in front of your valued inner circle and clients.

Anne Marie—once again your honesty and humour in applying your exquisite knowledge of the Queen's English are appreciated and loved. It was during our regular morning walks, where I shared, mused and debriefed many of the concepts in this book. Thank you.

Emma McGeorge—you continue to be the inspiration for much of my writing as I strive to create a better corporate working environment for everyone and, particularly, for you. I love you, my darling girl.

And finally, there is *nothing* I could do in my professional or personal life without the loving support of my husband, Steve. Our location has changed since the last time I wrote acknowledgements for a book, but nothing else has. You are still of service. You still swap out empty cups of tea and bring me snacks without my noticing. I'm still blessed. Thank you, my love.

Introduction

In 2020, Kim, like many workers around the world, found herself either in lockdown or being encouraged to work from home as authorities tried to get a handle on the pandemic.

Based in Victoria, she experienced one of Australia's toughest and longest lockdowns as it affected not just her but her family.

Prior to the pandemic, she would take her three-year-old son to day care. Mornings were chaotic for everyone. A far from relaxed breakfast, often eaten on the run, was followed by a half-crazed drive for the drop-off and the daily heartbreak of her son crying and clinging to her legs.

When lockdown hit and she had to work from home, Kim had time to walk her son to day care because she no longer had to commute. The tears and clinging stopped immediately. The dawdling morning walk allowed for a slower and calmer transition.

Kim had been refunded her commute time. The two hours a day gifted to her by COVID-19 restrictions were hers to use however she wished. She could simply have continued the upsetting morning routine, but she decided instead to spend the time wisely, and the return on that investment was huge.

If you were affected by lockdown, or had to work from home, how did you spend the commute time that was refunded to you?

Let's pause for a moment and do the maths. A commute of around one hour each way was common. Two hours' travel a day translated into ten hours a week that weren't spent in a car or on public transport. That's a whole extra day saved! Even if you caught the train and worked for part of the commute, the time saved was still yours to spend as you chose.

If I had asked you in 2019 what you would do with an extra day every week, how would you have answered?

You might have said you'd spend more time with your kids, read more, meal plan for the week, take up a hobby, study remotely or learn to navigate the new world in which many people work from home. Or maybe you would have said you'd simply catch up on sleep.

I don't think any of you would have said you would fill the saved time with more email and work-based projects.

Unfortunately, however, many of us perpetuated our already hectic lifestyles. Instead of recognising the time refund as a gift, we simply absorbed it back into our busy, out-of-control, overwhelmed lives. This meant many of us were more exhausted than when we commuted.

This book will help you take back time, get a refund if you will, build a time margin into your world so you are not operating constantly at 100 per cent–plus capacity, and rack up some room to move, breathe and think!

How good does that sound!?

People constantly tell me they are tired, exhausted and overwhelmed. They can't keep up with the pressures of modern-day living.

It's like we are always 'on' and have no idea how to hit the off switch—we don't even know there is one!

In Australia we work 3.2 billion hours a year in unpaid overtime, we have 134 million days of accrued annual leave, and 3.8 million of us don't take lunch breaks. And 7.4 million Australians don't get enough sleep.

We seem to have become 'rest resistant'. We are addicted to being busy and it's preventing us from getting the rest we need to perform at our best.

Wellbeing and productivity adviser Thea O'Connor reminds us, 'The simple fact is, if you don't give your brain a break you'll start to work more slowly and you'll make more errors.'

One of the things I learned in 2020 was that I didn't have to be 'on' all the time. I could actually organise my life so I started my first meeting at a time that suited me and I delivered sessions and workshops at a time that suited me.

I'm not sure why it took a pandemic for me to make that connection, but here I am. I spent a year protecting approximately 15 per cent of every day for time to think. I took time to reflect on what my customers needed rather than on what I was currently selling them. I spent time reading lots of articles online about what others were saying, and I began to craft my own story about what I had to offer. It led me to initiatives I had never thought of before. An Instagram account called 'Daily dose of Donna' provided simple tips and pick-me-ups for people in lockdown. I gained a heap of followers very quickly, and from those tips I began to develop programs that led me to a dozen new clients.

I believe that's why my practice was able not just to survive when others were folding or struggling, but to grow in a number of different directions. The investment of time saved gave me the ability to take advantage of opportunities.

For Kim and her son, that means never going back to the way things were before the pandemic. She considers the time she spends with him on the walk to the day-care centre sacrosanct and immovable.

That's my wish for everyone reading this book. I hope that by the time you've finished reading it you'll have implemented some simple strategies that will give you both the capacity and the space to think, breathe, work and enjoy your life even more.

Are you ready to see how?

How to use this book

This book mirrors the way I run my webinars, workshops, corporate programs and hands-on sessions. It is practical and easy to read and navigate, so you can quickly implement real yet simple changes in the way you work.

It isn't a hefty tome that you'll have trouble carrying around, or that you'll leave on your bedside table to gather coffee-cup stains. Rather, it offers quick tips, real-life stories, lots of no-nonsense advice, questions to encourage you to reflect on how you're working now and how you could improve, and exercises to help you implement the changes you want to make.

My suggestion for working through this book is to keep it simple and achievable. Start small and work your way up to the bigger concepts. Read the book and choose one or two things that resonate strongly with you, and start to action those immediately. (You will thank me for this when you see how simple it really is.)

Part I is all about why we need to take back time and how we collect our 1-Day Refund on the week. We will learn why 85 per cent is the limit we should be working towards (not 100 per cent or, dare I say, 120 per cent). We should all have a 15 per cent buffer in our lives for capacity and space.

Part II introduces strategies to help you spend your time saved wisely and to award yourself a daily refund. This will give you the capacity and space required to take advantage of opportunities to think and make great decisions, and to respond positively and proactively to changing conditions.

As you read, you will find I can be a little irreverent at times—because life and work are way too important to be taken too seriously. And reading a book should be a pleasure, not a pain!

So please read, implement, experiment and have fun being more productive!

PART I

WHY WE NEED TO TAKE BACK TIME

Resources and energy are needed for growth; this applies to pretty much any area of our world where we want to grow or get better. It is true for communities, for individuals and for the natural environment.

And I'm not just referring to physical growth. I'm also talking about emotional and intellectual growth.

In science, this is referred to as a finite-time singularity. In a nutshell, unbounded growth demands either infinite resources and energy or a major paradigm shift. Without either, collapse is inevitable.

So tell me, how much longer can you go on before you exhaust your resources and energy, or you undertake a paradigm shift?

I'm not even asking for a major shift. Simply think about where you can refund yourself only 15 per cent of your time and resources across a range of aspects of your life to create some space that will allow you to be the truly adaptive organism you have evolved to be. Following a few simple principles will gain you one full extra day in your week.

But you don't have to believe me! There are a number of real-world examples where a 15 per cent buffer or margin is considered optimal operating capacity.

Capacity utilisation (mostly used in manufacturing) measures the difference between production and production capability. Accounting for the fact that it is unlikely that an economy or company will function at 100 per cent capacity, 85 per cent is considered optimal. This provides a 15 per cent buffer against setbacks like equipment malfunction or resource shortages.

Olympians and professional sportspeople, too, know they will perform better at 85 per cent because they are more relaxed and can optimise muscle strength.

Hugh Jackman, in his preparation for and performance in the role of Wolverine, aimed to expend no more than 85 per cent of his energy, in the knowledge this would enable him to function optimally over extended production periods.

If we are to keep our own performance levels high and to optimise our resources and systems, we should be aiming for a maximum energy expenditure of 85 per cent.

This 15 per cent margin might seem arbitrary, or too little, and in many ways it's more about what happens in our heads than about watching the clock. Strive to feel as though you are performing at a steady pace, always with this tiny bit of room to breathe, not as though you are constantly catching up or struggling. You will feel in control instead of overwhelmed and exhausted from pushing yourself (or those around you) too far.

Of course, there will always be things outside your control: traffic jams, flight delays and other unexpected obstacles. Building in a 15 per cent buffer means you'll have greater capacity to manage disruptions.

This is how I arrived at the 1-Day Refund: 15 per cent of 7 is … 1! By applying some simple techniques and looking to shave 15 per cent off where you can, every week you can take back a whole day in your life!

Let's now explore this in more detail.

CHAPTER 1
We're busy addicts

We are all living in an epidemic of urgency and busyness. Unless we are flat out, working ridiculous hours, we are judged, and we often judge ourselves, as lazy or unproductive.

My friend Sharon is a senior manager in a large professional services organisation. She is also studying part time and has a seven-year-old daughter. She arrives for work most days around 8.15 am after the school drop-off and leaves around 5.30 pm most afternoons to get back to afterschool care by the 6.30 pm deadline. Some days are pretty tight!

Despite this, she is productive and effective, but not always super social at work. Her boss, having noticed her arrival and departure times, recently pulled her aside and said, 'People are noticing that you come in around 8.15 and leave around 5.30 most days. I've noticed as well. This would indicate to me that you don't have enough to do.'

To her credit, Sharon didn't react badly (I might have). She asked, 'What is it that others, or you, feel I'm not doing? Have I missed some deadlines or is my work not up to scratch?' Her boss said, 'No, no, your work is fine. I get great feedback. It's just that others seem to work longer hours.'

Sharon replied,

> **I'm focused and efficient. I have to be. I have to be able to hold the job down and get home to my family. When the quality or quantity of my output starts to be less than what you are wanting, please let me know and we can have a discussion about my work hours then.**

I'm thinking she may have looked like a woman on the edge, because her boss agreed and backed away ... slowly.

But let's not blame Sharon's boss. Urgency is the new black. 'Busy' is the natural response to 'How's work?' The effect is cultures that pride themselves on 'fast-moving' or 'adaptive' workplaces. But they are often white-collar sweat shops, pushing people beyond their limits, and the result is burnout.

> **Matthew Bidwell, from the University of Pennsylvania's Wharton School, says of managers that when they can't measure outputs easily, they will measure inputs, such as how long you are spending at work.**

Trading time for money

Sharon told me that in her workplace, people are often judged not by their outputs but by how many hours they spend in the office. Some were even careful to arrive five minutes before, and to leave five minutes after, their boss. I'm sure you have a similar story—most of us do!

My brother, for example, was once chastised in a performance review because he was 'too cheerful and didn't exhibit signs of stress', which indicated to his boss that he didn't have enough to do. He couldn't possibly be adding value *and* remain cheerful! My brother left that job shortly after and was told by colleagues that people kept discovering how much he did in a day. 'Bill used to do that' was the answer to just about every question asked about tasks in the department.

The notion that busyness, franticness and stress are indicators of hard work and productivity has been around for over 2000 years. It seems that we are somehow wrong if we aren't feeling these things. The Stoic philosopher Seneca, author of *On the Shortness of Life*, arguably the first ever management self-help book, argued:

People are frugal in guarding their personal property; but as soon as it comes to squandering time, they are most wasteful of the one thing in which it is right to be stingy.

The industrial revolution specifically linked time to money as the advent of artificial lighting enabled 10- to 16-hour workdays. It wasn't until Henry Ford introduced the eight-hour workday, and profits increased exponentially, that people started to think differently about productivity by the hour. His profitable methods, in effect, refunded two to eight hours to his workers every day.

We are also driven by a work ethic deeply rooted in Judaeo-Christian traditions that persuades us that to be 'idle' is to be 'ungodly'.

Love not sleep, lest you come to poverty; open your eyes, and you will have plenty of bread.
Proverbs 20:13

In a culture that values hard work and productivity, we feel we are 'winning' when we are going hard all the time. Because being busy increases our level of (self-)importance and can become addictive, we may feel guilty or ashamed when we aren't busy doing stuff.

So we have a bit of conditioning to undo!

Instead of trading time for money, we need to trade energy for impact.

For example, we are all familiar with the model that says I give you x hours of my time in exchange for y dollars. But what if we instead focused on the idea that I give you energy, value and impact in return for dollars?

Instead of thinking about how many hours I need to put in, I think about exchanging the most valuable and impactful work each day.

Begin by asking yourself, where will I get the best return on my energy investment?

Reframe laziness

If you have a dog or a cat, watch them. They spend most of their time sleeping, with intermittent breaks for eating, pooping and running after a ball or a bird.

I think it's time to reframe 'laziness' and to enjoy life's pauses. Let's not be like Nathan Hubbard, former CEO of Ticketmaster, who in this tweet seems to be encouraging people to go hard over the holiday period.

Nathan Hubbard
@NathanCHubbard

Whatever you're hustling for, take note: most people/ companies are shut down until '18. This means you get 2 extra weeks to outwork your competition. That's 3.8% more time. For perspective: Usain Bolt won his gold medals running 1.2% faster. These 2 weeks are a gift. Get to work.

9:22 AM • Dec 19, 2017 from Los Angeles, CA

For years researchers have proved time and time again the positive impact of restful activities:

» Daydreaming, and even boredom, promote creative thinking.

» Discovering non-work-related activities that both rejuvenate and excite you will provide the energy you need when it's time to get down to work. They also create an awesome contrast frame so you'll enjoy work-related activities even more!

» Being in flow: Mihaly Csíkszentmihályi coined this term in the 1970s for what happens when we become 'so immersed in a feeling of energized focus, full involvement, and enjoyment in the process of the activity that we lose sense of space and time'. And we get more done! Up to 500 per cent more, according to a 10-year McKinsey study.

» Socialising: We get cognitive boosts from social interactions and we also experience higher levels of intellectual performance.

» Disconnecting from work: Those of us who are able to disconnect from work are healthier, more engaged when we are at work and less prone to procrastination.

Being less busy isn't the issue. The real opportunity here is to take time out. To stop and take stock of where you are at and make some decisions about how you want to work.

Without some level of mastery and control over your time, at best you will lose opportunities and at worst you will become ill.

STOP AND THINK

Studies of brainwaves show us that creativity, innovation, inspiration and intuition are only available to us when our brain is in certain states of consciousness.

Have you ever heard someone say, 'I just can't think clearly!' or 'I can't make sense of this!' or 'I just don't have the bandwidth for this'? Just ask the parents of a newborn who are not getting enough sleep. Typically, this is because they cannot access sufficiently the brainwave that helps you feel centred, relaxed and creative!

The Dutch principle of *niksen* means to slow down and opt out of productivity expectations. The idea is you take a big breath, pause, and give your mind and body a chance to rest and reset.

Writers and philosophers have been talking and writing about this for centuries. It's no secret that our aha! moments often happen when we're resting.

In *Awakening the Mind*, Anna Wise explains that while we rarely use just one kind of brainwave at a time, each has its own job or characteristics. For example:

» Beta brainwaves are the most commonly used, and they're the fastest. Typically, these are accessed in a waking state of consciousness or when you're thinking—like now, as you read this book. They help us manage everyday things like driving a car, making judgements and remembering what we need to do. They are responsible for analytical thinking and problem-solving.

» Alpha brainwaves are the next fastest and are typically present when we are in a state of relaxation or distant awareness, such as when we are daydreaming. You can access alpha waves through anything that 'zones you out', like watching TV, working on a hobby or even taking a long drive. It's where positive thinking, stress reduction and accelerated learning lives. Its most useful function is to create a bridge between the conscious and subconscious parts of your mind. It's why you remember dreams.

» Theta brainwaves are accessed when you sleep, and more specifically in the rapid eye movement (REM) state. It's how we transfer things from short-term to long-term memory. If you meditate, you will be aware of the blissful feelings that result when you are able to access this state of consciousness. This is where aha! experiences live. It's where healing begins and it fosters feelings of deep inner peace. And it's also where creativity lives.

» Delta brainwaves are the slowest and they belong mainly in the realm of the unconscious mind. They are present when all other frequencies are turned off, giving you the chance to get a good night's sleep. They can sometimes be present in waking states, showing up as intuition, empathy and instinct. When people say that, despite the evidence, 'I just knew ...', they are probably accessing delta brainwaves.

In a nutshell, if you are not accessing these brainwaves at the appropriate time, you will not have access to the ability to be creative, innovative and intuitive.

So we need to STOP!

To sum up chapter 1 in a sentence: we are told that we need to operate at 100 per cent capacity all the time, and anything less is less than optimal—but *it's not true!*

In chapter 2 we learn that there are forms of capacity other than working flat out at 100 per cent!

Begin to reframe boredom as necessary rest. It's okay to have nothing to do.

15% TIP

Wakeup call

'I can't afford to get sick!' I'm sure we've all said this from time to time. It was Deborah's catchcry. Her household was a typically busy one with two working parents and school-aged kids.

Deborah is a nursing unit manager at a major hospital and she was 100 per cent 'on' pretty much from the moment she arrived at work until her shift finished. She prided herself on being able to nip illness in the bud! Until she experienced an immune system breakdown due to prolonged stress and overload and the varicella virus, or shingles, reactivated in her body.

Because shingles is contagious, she had to take time off work. It was the first time in her life she had taken the time to heal and she saw it as the wakeup call it was. It was time to create some capacity in her world not just to slow down but to give her body a chance to rest. She began to focus on developing the abilities of her team so the workload was more evenly distributed, and this gave her the space to think and lead.

At home, because in the early stages her shingles had been quite severe, the family had had to step up. Once she got better, she didn't take back all the responsibilities she had relinquished.

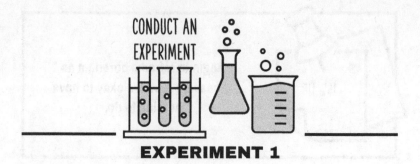

EXPERIMENT 1

Encourage your mind to wander:

1. Grab a notebook (or paper) and pen and set a timer for 10 minutes. (A 30-minute stretch works best, but baby steps, eh?)

2. Write whatever comes into your head. Just release the flow of consciousness. It doesn't matter if what you write doesn't make sense, or even if you admit, 'I'm writing stuff but I don't know why and this feels stupid, and now I'm thinking about giraffes.' Keep writing until the alarm goes off.

3. If you can eventually get to a full 30 minutes each day, particularly when you first wake, you'll notice the benefit.

This exercise is based on Julia Cameron's 'Morning Pages' from *The Artist's Way*: 'They are about anything and everything that crosses your mind—and they are for your eyes only. Morning Pages provoke, clarify, comfort, cajole, prioritise and synchronise the day at hand.'

Remembering that daydreaming and boredom can be necessary to promote creativity, are you actually bored or is this essential downtime?

How could looking after yourself enable you to serve others better?

What mindfulness technique might you start with? You might begin by simply sitting with stillness and observing the detail around you.

CHAPTER 2

We need the capacity to adapt

I was at a meeting recently—an in-person live meeting (rare in 2021)—and I noticed a behavioural pattern as people got cups of tea or coffee and moved around the room. Those who had filled their cup to the brim had to concentrate hard to avoid spilling any before they reached the meeting table. Those who had filled to around 85 per cent capacity were easily able to return to the table without spilling anything. They were also able to multitask by chatting with others. One even waved her cup and saucer around as she gestured. Didn't spill a drop!

Seems pretty obvious really, doesn't it? But I'm not so sure we think about this when it comes to our minds and our work.

My client Jessica is a senior executive in a large global organisation. Her work is important and demanding. She's the mother of two early teenage daughters, and her husband also works.

Jessica has a short fuse. She has been known to snap at people (including family) when it may not have been the best response. Her husband has learned that one little thing can cause a massive explosion! She is frequently short of breath when she speaks, and she speaks so quickly she stumbles over her words a lot. She always seems to be running late or barely on time. She forgets stuff and often has to backtrack.

She told me how she once arrived at the airport for a business trip, only to discover when she reached for ID to board her flight that she had forgotten her wallet. She had no credit card to pay to exit the car park and go home to fetch her wallet. It was a disaster.

She has many stories like this—heading to the theatre and leaving the tickets at home, or going to the wrong restaurant because she hadn't paid attention to the address, or getting there and finding she hadn't booked.

Now, to be fair to Jessica, this doesn't happen all the time. She does her job very well and rarely lets things slip through the cracks at work. If you notice my examples, it's mostly her personal life that suffers. This is because Jessica is operating at more than 100 per cent capacity and she is spilling stuff all over the place!

When you operate at 100 per cent capacity it doesn't take much to send things off the rails.

Are you at max capacity?

Let's face it. S#!& happens! My dad always had a 'rainy day' approach to life. He was always early, always had a bit of extra cash squirreled away and worried only about things he could control or influence. When you are running late, it seems every traffic light is against you. When you have built in ample time, the traffic parts like the Red Sea!

If you are like Jessica—and many of us are—you need to find ways to lengthen your fuse by making space in your life so you are able to respond effectively to unexpected challenges.

In *The 7 Habits of Highly Effective People*, Stephen Covey discusses something similar to our fuse-lengthening idea. In 'Habit 1: Be Proactive' he suggests we create space between stimulus and response. When the space is too small (short fuse), we overreact to the stimulus of a minor inconvenience. When the space is larger (long fuse), we have time to be proactive.

To do this, we need to create more capacity!

Capacity is both:

» the maximum amount that a 'vessel' can contain

» the amount that something can produce.

This book is about this second element: acknowledging and leveraging our ability to produce stuff. To do that we need *energy* and *time* (figure 2.1, overleaf):

» **Energy.** Like a battery, we need to have some charge. We've all felt what it's like when we've almost run out of juice. We may have some capacity left, but not enough to do the important stuff as effectively as we'd like. It's like running on empty.

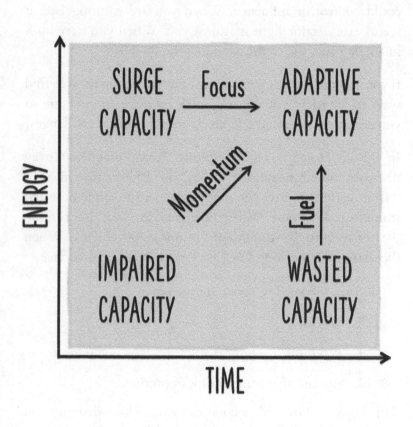

Figure 2.1: the energy/time matrix

» **Time.** This is arguably the most valuable commodity in the world. Let's face it, if we could package and sell time, we'd be billionaires several times over. Without time, we can't really get anything done.

When we don't have enough time or energy to do the important things in our world, we have *impaired* capacity. It's like working on a treadmill, expending energy but never getting anywhere. Work can feel like this. We use up time and energy on mundane activities and have nothing left for people and activities that really matter. What we need is momentum—something, ANYTHING, to get moving.

When we have a lot of time but not much energy, we have *wasted* capacity. You know you are here when you have a lot to do but cannot muster the energy to make it happen. You have hit your energy limit. No judgement, but do you know what it's like to have a book to write, yet you cannot muster the energy to get off the couch, so you binge watch Netflix? #askingforafriend.

For what it's worth, I think a lot of unproductive busy work happens because of wasted capacity. I have time on my hands, and not much to do, so I'll 'potter around without any intention'.

Here we need fuel. Whatever it takes to give us energy. Fuel might take the form of food, exercise or time spent with someone who inspires us, or it could be emotional fuel, like prayer, meditation or time for contemplation.

When we have too much time on our hands, we can sometimes turn our attention inwards, which can exacerbate wasted capacity by leading to rumination, anxiety and depression.

When we have a lot of energy but not a lot of time, we have *surge* capacity. This is our modus operandi most of the time. If you are feeling out of control, rushed, just scraping by, getting stuff done but only just, then it's likely you are operating at surge capacity.

We all have a measure of surge capacity. It's what we access when we are already at 100 per cent and we need a little more when the unexpected happens. It's only meant as a short-term response, however. We shouldn't be operating that way all the time.

Hospitals are a great illustration of the management of surge capacity. If a major disaster happens (an extreme weather event, say), they are able to call on off-duty team members to surge in response.

When I worked for an airline years ago, we were trained to be 'surge responders' in the event of an accident. We were advised where we needed to go and what our roles were so we could quickly get on board.

This is where this book can help you most. It's about budgeting your time so you are not constantly surging. When you have a lot of energy and a lot of time, you have *adaptive* capacity. This is the ability to take advantage of change, to respond to disruptive circumstances positively and to cope when the unexpected happens.

You will recognise people in your life who have adaptive capacity. They're the ones who remain calm under pressure. They never appear stressed or challenged when things don't go well.

Broadly, and more scientifically, adaptive capacity can be described as the ability or capacity of a system to modify or change its characteristics or behaviour in response to existing or anticipated external stresses. The term is used often to describe adaptations to climate change.

This is not new thinking. Darwin's theory of natural selection argues that a species' adaptive capacity influences the extent to which it is able to adapt and thrive in a changed environment.

For our purposes, it simply points to whether we have the mental, physical and temporal space to respond positively when things don't go according to plan, and even to seize opportunities that may exist as a result of new conditions.

What is the right refund of time between wasted and adaptive capacity? The answer is 15 per cent. In chapter 3 we'll learn more about this magic number.

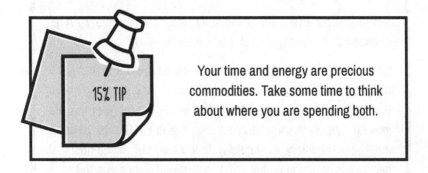

15% TIP

Your time and energy are precious commodities. Take some time to think about where you are spending both.

Stagekings

Stagekings is an Australian company launched in 2015 by husband-and-wife team Jeremy and Tabitha Fleming.

They were motived by the idea that the Australian event industry, particularly the music and entertainment sector, 'could be enhanced by introducing custom-designed decorated stages, similar to some of the incredible large-scale designs that are often seen across the European music festival scene'.

The idea quickly took off, and soon Stagekings were designing and building some of the largest custom stages and event structures in the country.

On 13 March 2020, they were halfway through building a massive set for Formula 1 in Melbourne as well as the set for Channel 9's *Ninja Warrior*, and having discussions with dozens of event companies and agencies about creating some really awesome stuff, when their world collapsed.

Like just about everyone in Australia, they will remember Friday, 13 March 2020, for the rest of their careers.

It was the day the prime minister announced measures that led to the immediate shutdown of their industry by placing uncompromising restrictions on all public events. The events sector was the first national industry to completely fall over due to the COVID-19 crisis, and it happened very, very quickly. In the space of just 48 hours, all their bookings for the rest of 2020 and beyond were cancelled.

That's when Stagekings decided to get creative and brought the team together to brainstorm their survival strategy.

They asked themselves, 'What do people need at a time like this?' Recognising that tens of thousands of people would have to start working from home with almost immediate effect, they put their specialised cutting equipment to work making work-from-home desks.

It was an instant hit, resulting in the manufacture of nearly 10 000 products, and they increased their workforce from 12 to more than 50 people working across four states.

Stagekings' ability to surge (bring everyone in) and then adapt (come up with a plan) has become legendary.

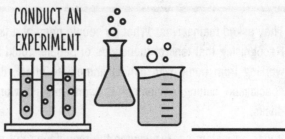

EXPERIMENT 2

There's no surer sign of high stress levels brought on by being in a constant state of surge than what we've described as a short fuse. In a world in which everything is urgent, there will always be plenty of opportunities for tempers to flare.

The antidote is patience. But first let's check in to see how long your fuse is. Answer the following questions *honestly* (no-one else will see your answers). Put the number next to your answer in the column to the right. Then add them up and check your response below.

You're stuck in traffic after a long day at work. What are you doing?	
1. Singing out loud	
2. Zoning out	
3. Freaking out	
4. Cursing heaven and earth	
You just got dumped in the worst possible way. What do you reach for?	
1. Google—to search for a month-long meditation retreat	
2. A stiff drink	

3. A phone to call a friend	
4. A broom to clean up the broken shards of the glass you threw across the room	
When things aren't going well, what activity do you find the most energising?	
1. Yoga	
2. Walking or jogging	
3. Breaking things	
4. Grabbing a gun and shooting something	
You burned the toast and you're out of bread. Where does the burnt toast end up?	
1. In the bin—you'll have cereal instead	
2. In the bin—you'll grab something on the way to work	
3. In your stomach—you'll eat it out of spite	
4. On the floor—to be stomped on	
What prompts you to swear under your breath?	
1. A near-miss car accident	
2. Stubbing your toe	
3. Your computer freezes, again	
4. Just about anything	
When is it okay to use your car horn?	
1. When an accident is imminent	
2. When someone cuts in front of you	
3. When someone takes longer than three seconds to move at a green light	
4. When someone crosses the street too slowly	

You're finishing something on your computer when the flight attendant asks you to put it away. How do you react?	
1. Smile and put it away instantly	
2. Be a little bothered but put it away	
3. Roll your eyes and scowl, but eventually put it away	
4. Angrily ask why, berate them for asking, arguing that the plane will be fine whether your device is on or off	
It's no use crying over spilt milk	
1. True	
2. Depends how badly you wanted the milk	
3. Do you know how much milk costs!?	
4. False	
You get an email from your boss that really bugs you. How do you respond?	
1. Pause and pick up the phone; it's likely to be a misunderstanding	
2. Reply with a question for clarity	
3. Kill 'em with kindness	
4. Let them have it with both barrels	
You're on a long flight and there's a kicking toddler sitting behind you. What do you do?	
1. Ignore it—it's the way of the world	
2. Ask the flight attendant to do something about it	
3. Give the parent a 'look'	
4. Tell the parents to control their kid	

Total Score: _____

Score of 10–15: Your fuse is so long it never seems to light the bomb.

Centred—Not much fazes you. You guide your ship well through stormy seas. It takes a big wave to rock you, but with a little work you always find calm waters.

Score of 16–25: There's time between the fuse being lit and choosing your response.

Composed—You are mostly settled and while you may get a little flustered, you generally have the wherewithal to breathe deep and remain poised.

Score of 26–35: You must work hard to manage your short fuse.

Controlled—You have to try hard to control your responses. For the most part you succeed in keeping your fraying temper under wraps.

Score of 36–40: There's almost no space between the stimulus and your response.

Crazed—You're like a firecracker. The slightest upset can provoke a nuclear response.

PAUSE FOR A MOMENT ⏸

What daily activity could you undertake to improve your patience? Think about pausing before responding, or acknowledging what is bothering you is out of your control.

What happens just before your fuse ignites? Pay attention to the warning signs.

What's the long view of where you are at right now? Whatever you are dealing with is a short-term situation that will likely be resolved in the longer term.

CHAPTER 3

We perform best with less

I hope you're beginning to understand you could work more effectively if, instead of constantly operating at 100 per cent capacity or more, you aimed for about 85 per cent, giving you a one-day refund.

In a nutshell, this margin is the difference between your total capacity and how much capacity you are using.

Olympian Carl Lewis, the nine-time gold medallist sprinter, was known as a 'master finisher'. Interestingly for us, he was considered to be a slow starter. In a 100-metre sprint, he was often either last or second to last at the 40-metre mark, but breezed past other competitors by the finish line. Contrary to common sense, he did nothing special towards the end. His breathing and form remained the same throughout the race. While other runners were clearly having to push harder at the end—clenching their fists, scrunching their faces—Carl Lewis looked exactly the same when he won the race as he had at the start.

It came to be understood later that while others were performing at full throttle, Carl Lewis was running at 85 per cent from start to finish.

Think about your eight-hour workday. (You might think I'm dreaming, but stay with me on this.) Your eight hours are your total capacity. If you plan to use all those working hours, you aren't leaving yourself any margin.

What do you need a margin for? Think about the last time you put your head down to dedicate yourself to getting something done. How many times were you interrupted? And how much longer did it take to complete what you needed to do?

How often do we truly do eight hours of solid work in an eight-hour time frame?

That's why we need a margin. If we plan to operate at 85 per cent capacity, we would be doing just under seven hours' work in an eight-hour day. That way, if something unexpected comes up (and it will) we can handle it.

While not all of us work a seven-day week, with a few nudges and savings, we could still take back a whole day to give us some room to move. If we underestimate how long something will take (and we will), we can still meet our target for the day.

In the book he wrote with Amos Tversky, *Thinking, Fast and Slow*, Daniel Kahneman first coined the term 'the planning fallacy'. As he explained, we tend to be over-optimistic about the time needed to complete a task.

The more we become conscious of our own working styles and the volume of work we need to complete, the more we become conscious of our capacity and what our margins are, and the less likely we are to fall for the planning fallacy.

Your capacity is a product of your time, energy and attention.

While energy and attention are a little harder to quantify than time available, it's your margin that will have the biggest impact on them. A 15 per cent margin gives you the space and additional resources to avoid burnout and take care of yourself.

What if you were to focus 100 per cent on fewer things? Imagine if you were able to fully complete one project or significant piece of work every day for 30 days. Whoa! Would you be in a better position than you are in now?

Deadlines are useful, but it's your capacity that will drive your projects.

Small things, consistently

If behaviour scientist BJ Fogg's *Tiny Habits: Why Starting Small Makes Lasting Change Easy* teaches us anything, it's that getting small things done, consistently over time, will have the greatest impact on our results and productivity.

If you work at 85 per cent capacity and focus 100 per cent on the task at hand, chances are you will get more consistent results.

In just about every situation I can think of, the people who are regarded as the 'most successful' at 'getting a lot done' aren't necessarily those with the greatest ideas. It's rather that they execute a somewhat ordinary idea really well. It's the difference between authors who actually write books and musicians who actually perform on stage and those who only dream about it. People who achieve great results typically do it over time, consistently. And they work at 85 per cent capacity with 100 per cent focus.

Give yourself a break

You'll do far better if, rather than operating flat out at 100 per cent capacity all the time, you perform below your peak capacity, thereby giving yourself some breathing room to relax as well as some capacity to surge when necessary.

For example, when building a business, giving 100 per cent would mean working 20 hours a day, seven days a week. Clearly, this isn't sustainable.

I know it feels wrong to put in less effort, but rest and relaxation are essential elements in producing your best work. Studies have shown that trying too hard at work doesn't usually result in positive career outcomes and is actually detrimental to one's career.

Whether it's work, a hobby, or even your social life, dialling back the intensity of your effort may turn out to be a good thing.

What would happen if your goal was to enjoy what you did, rather than performing at full throttle until your head becomes a pressure cooker ready to explode?

For example, my weekly goal for my book isn't to produce a specific word count. That's too big an expectation and will suck the joy out of the writing process. My goal each week is to write a chapter that's readable and doesn't waste my readers' time. Every week I give myself some leeway so it doesn't become exhausting. This helps me relax and write better.

Aiming to perform at 85 per cent not only takes the pressure off; it allows you to play the game for longer, giving you an advantage over others. So pop the kettle on and make a cuppa. Take a few hours to sit quietly, relax and enjoy this book. This is your 15 per cent refund for today!

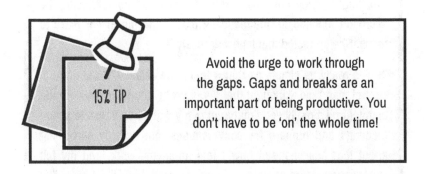

15% TIP

Avoid the urge to work through the gaps. Gaps and breaks are an important part of being productive. You don't have to be 'on' the whole time!

Rest for change

Jenny is a change-management coach and facilitator who also teaches leadership development. She first heard about the 1-Day Refund when I spoke at a conference in early 2021, and she immediately began to apply the principles that would enable her to give herself a 15 per cent refund every day.

(continued)

Initially she aimed to set aside only one hour a month (she called it the one fortieth rule), and, while she consistently achieved this, she didn't notice an overall change in how her world felt or any improvement in her productivity.

She encouraged her clients to do the same, especially those who were busy and were being pulled from pillar to post with no time to shape their work or have the conversations essential to her methodology. She believes change happens one conversation at a time and that leaders need to be conscious of how they are preparing for those conversations.

She began trying the 1-Day Refund system on herself, using the Microsoft function to automatically block out time in her diary to focus. She protected that time vigorously:

'It was really as simple as that. I feel more relaxed. I feel more in control than I did. I thought that I was pretty good. I'm a very good planner and a really good manager of my diary. I do pause to shape meetings and prepare for conversations, but actually something about that has changed how I feel about my work, and my felt experience is more at ease and more relaxed. I feel like I know I've got the space I need.'

Jenny's story is about how to build in more adaptive capacity because things do happen and change is often stressful. Those of us who are operating at surge capacity don't have the space to ask, 'What's the opportunity here?' or, 'This is interesting—I wonder what it means' or, 'Let's explore this. I'm curious about the impact.'

Building in a 15 per cent refund of time allows you to respond to people and be available when and where you are needed.

CONDUCT AN
EXPERIMENT

EXPERIMENT 3

Actor Patrick Stewart often has to be up, showered and ready to go for a 5 am pickup. He has built his adaptive capacity into the morning by setting his alarm for 4 am, giving him time to make a cup of tea and go back to bed and read.

> **I don't read the paper because it makes me angry. I don't read my emails because it usually makes me anxious and gets my mind going. I read a book. The kind of book that you pick up when you go on vacation. The 'I've got nothing to do book'.**

He reads in the morning because he fears the day will get away from him and he won't have time for it in the evening.

I suggest there's a secondary gain. Imagine starting every day in the relaxed frame of mind usually associated with being on vacation instead of dashing out of the blocks on high alert.

What kinds of books do you like to read on holiday? For me it's science fiction, or what I like to call 'lose yourself in them' books. It has to be the kind of book that signals to your brain that you are on vacation.

» Put that book beside your bed before you go to sleep.

» Set your alarm for 30 minutes earlier than usual.

» Pick up that vacation book and read for half an hour.

» Try this for 30 days and take note of what you feel.

37

PAUSE FOR A MOMENT

Measuring effort can be tricky. For example, how do you know you are operating at 85 per cent capacity? The best way to measure effort is to check your state of mind.

How are you feeling? How would you describe your mood at any given moment? How are you feeling more generally? Good: unstressed, on track, focused, happy with your progress? Or bad: stressed, out of control, scattered and running behind?

Pay attention to the pattern of these feelings. Feeling bad too many days in a row may indicate that you are pushing too hard and exceeding 100 per cent capacity.

PART II

HOW TO SPEND YOUR TIME WISELY

People tell me all the time that they feel out of control or overwhelmed and are worried about, or actually failing at, the important things. We need to get out of this vicious cycle and into a more positive one.

When it comes to finding our refund, we need to look at both our mental and our physical capacity—our brain space and our living space. And we need to find balance in both our professional and our personal lives in order to access more capacity.

What can we do to give ourselves more capacity? We need to apply techniques across four aspects of our lives, as illustrated in figure A.

1. **Thinking space:** We can decelerate, decompress then decide what it is we need to do to move forward. We can cut through all the noise in our lives, get clear on our current state and make some decisions about where we should be spending our time. We need to take time out.

2. **Breathing space:** We can disengage from people and activities that create stress and anxiety, so we can devote more time to the important things in our world. Things that bring us happiness and joy. We need to let go.

3. **Living space:** We can think like a designer and design our spaces to be more functional and productive. We can declutter our spaces so we are not overwhelmed by our surroundings and decomplicate them to remove friction from how we move around our world. We need to free up our resources.

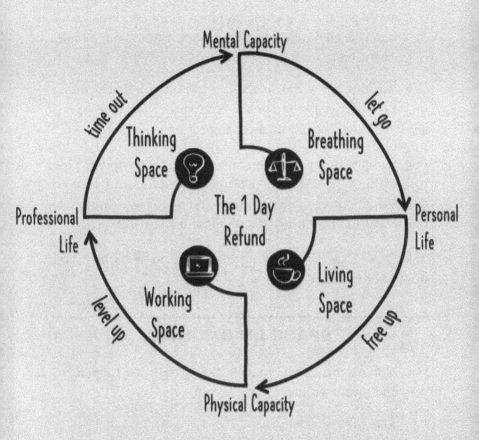

Figure A: space framework

4. **Working space:** We can define our vision of what we want our work and careers to be about. We can then defrag our working days, weeks and months by batching our work and creating larger chunks of space to do the more intense and impactful work. Finally, we can delegate to best lead both ourselves and our people. We need to level up.

We can start anywhere in the space framework, depending on where it is we need to create more space. The four aspects are interconnected; each has an impact on the others.

For example, if our living space is not conducive to thinking or breathing, then that's a great place to start. And without the thinking space to clarify our vision of our working space, our living and breathing spaces will also feel constricted.

Take a look at the following diagnostic to see where you might need to start.

SPACE DIAGNOSTIC

For each statement, ask yourself how often this happens to you, and give it a score:

1. Never

2. Rarely

3. Sometimes

4. Often

5. Always

Once you are done, check your score.

1. I feel overwhelmed and out of control.	
2. I'm being pulled in too many directions.	
3. I spend a lot of time trying to find things I've misplaced.	
4. I find I take work home, or into personal time.	
5. I have a lot to do and don't know where to start.	
6. I find myself rushing to meet deadlines.	
7. I don't have enough storage space for all my stuff.	
8. I struggle to manage competing priorities.	
9. I feel I'm neglecting the most important people in my world.	
10. Interruptions prevent me from focusing on what I should be doing.	
11. Tasks take me twice as long as I planned because I'm disorganised.	
12. I'm spending my time, money and energy on the wrong people or activities.	

Check your score:

Questions 1, 5 and 8 for your **thinking space** score	
Questions 2, 9 and 12 for your **breathing space** score	
Questions 3, 7 and 11 for your **living space** score	
Questions 4, 6 and 10 for your **working space** score	

This very simple tool guides you as you begin your journey and can help to determine the order in which you read the chapters that follow.

For example, a high score (over 10) would indicate you may have a problem. So start with the chapter that correlates with the statement that received the highest score and work your way through to the one that scored lowest.

If all your scores were similar, or if you simply prefer to read sequentially, then start at the beginning.

CHAPTER 4
Thinking space

In September 2018 I was struggling. I was staying up late playing catch-up with my ever-growing workload. I was short-tempered, cranky and sometimes unappreciative of my always-supportive husband. I could feel a growing distance between us as he tried to figure out how to help me. My physical health was suffering. I had gained weight and this was affecting my knees. My anxiety was at an all-time high and I believed I had no time to address the things that would help. I was dedicating all my time to my clients—great for them, but not sustainable in the long term.

I was sitting at the kitchen bench trying to complete a detailed PDF form from a client to get into their payment system for an upcoming project, and it was like the world went blurry and I found I couldn't read the document no matter how much I increased the zoom. I became hypersensitive to noise and snapped at my husband to turn everything off. To make matters worse, I just couldn't think! My normal smarts had deserted me.

I was having a full-blown anxiety attack and said through tears to my hubby, 'I can't do this anymore.'

He gave me a long hug, put the kettle on and said, 'It's time to slow down and stop.' I picked up a small red Moleskine notebook I had recently purchased for my growing collection of 'someday' notebooks and spent the next three hours drinking tea and quietly taking stock.

I made lists of things that needed to happen in the next two weeks and organised them according to their intensity and impact (I cover this in my book *The First 2 Hours*). I made decisions and set targets for personal activities like walking and eating, and for business-related ones like sales calls and financial targets. Immediately I felt myself regaining control.

Too often our systems are overrun with cortisol and adrenaline, which puts us in a state of heightened alert. Our bodies and brains think we are under threat, so we become disconnected from the frontal lobe, which is essential for executive function and our ability to think and problem-solve. Frankly, we are not in a fit state to do anything.

We can regain our sanity and sound judgement once we stop, take stock and create more thinking space so we can make decisions based on what we need to do to move forward.

Purple patches

When was the last time you had 'free time' in your diary? Most of the time we end up with a bit of free space by accident when an appointment is cancelled. And how good does that feel?

One of my clients identified these rare moments as 'purple patches'. I encouraged him to block out these patches so he could take advantage of them any time he liked! He colour-coded the time—in purple—in his calendar.

Another client recently told me, 'I don't know what I'd do with myself with all that spare time!' I asked, 'When a meeting is cancelled, what do you do?' She replied, 'I catch up on a whole bunch of stuff!' I said, 'Well, that's what you would do! First you would catch up, and then after a while your horizon of work would start to shift. Instead of playing catch-up, you would start to look a week ahead and get things ready, then maybe two weeks, then a month, then a quarter!'

And that's how this works. Blocking time out doesn't mean you do nothing; it means *you* decide what you want to do. You can use that time to your best advantage.

This time is for what *you* want to do. You are not beholden to anyone, and you don't have to have your game face on. If this time had a wardrobe it would be tracky dacks (or sweatpants) and ugg boots.

You shift from reacting to what has to be done right now, urgently, to being proactive and planning ahead.

This is what creates the appearance of cool, calm and collected. It also creates space to deal with any emergencies that may occur.

What will a 15 per cent refund look like in practical terms? We know it will give us an extra day in our week. That's not the only way of looking at it, though:

» In a year you'll get back 1.8 months (or 7.8 weeks).

» In a quarter—1.8 weeks.

» In a 20-day month—3 days.

» In a 40-hour work week—6 hours.

» In a seven-day week—1 day.

» In an 8-hour day—1.2 hours.

Which one feels doable to you? It's probably state- and context-dependent—meaning, how are you feeling and what do you need to get done? Some of these options may be outside your comfort zone and make you feel quite uncomfortable!

For example, blocking out almost eight weeks of the year to 'think' may seem extravagant and wasteful, unless you are writing a book or a dissertation, studying, business planning or making a significant change in your life. There's a reason why many professions encourage sabbaticals.

Taking about two weeks every quarter is accepted practice in education because we know that kids and students need a break from the effort of constant learning. Are adults any different?

Blocking out three days per month may soon start to feel appropriate in the corporate world. We can imagine marking it in our diary and using the time to take stock and do some decent planning.

Blocking out six hours a week, or 1.2 hours a day, is where many people land because it has the least perceived impact on others. We can imagine holding on to that space in our diaries and gaining more control.

Pick one and try it out!

Too often we let these things happen accidentally rather than intentionally.

As it happens, I'm writing this chapter because of some accidental down time. During March 2021, a massive rain-filled weather front moved across parts of New South Wales and southern Queensland, bringing everything to a halt. I was in Queensland to look at real estate, because we were planning a move, but road closures forced us into a form of lockdown, which provided me with a purple patch of several days. This space to stop and think and write was a gift!

Under normal circumstances, though, it's important that you block the time intentionally, and then choose what to do with it.

Figure 4.1 (overleaf) shows us what we need to do to take some time out and create more thinking space.

By making time to decelerate, decompress and decide, we are clearing thinking space, which will enable us to make better choices.

1. **Decelerating** is about slowing down or stopping, taking time out just to pause and be. You are off duty and beholden to no-one.

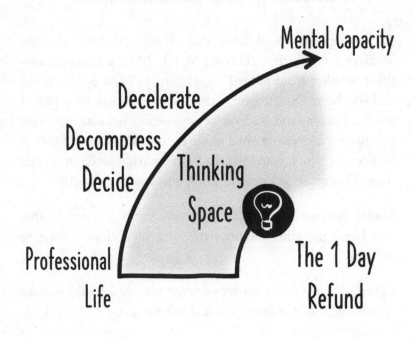

Figure 4.1: thinking space

2. **Decompressing** is about letting off the pressure. We all know what happens when pressure builds in any context. At best it triggers a malfunction, at worst an explosion! We can release the pressure in the brain by writing things down, removing the need to hold everything at front of mind.

3. **Deciding** can only happen once we have stopped and taken stock. It's a bit like cleaning out the pantry, wardrobe or garage. We generally get better results if we take everything out and put back only what needs to be there. Because there's always a bit of chaos before the feeling of control, it's important first to decelerate and decompress.

Decelerate

Do you ever just do nothing? No, really. Nothing. Perhaps sitting on the sofa and daydreaming, alone with your thoughts without the TV on or your phone in your hand? Chances are your answer is 'rarely or never'. We are accessible 24/7 and though we make sure our devices' batteries are fully charged, we rarely pay attention to our own.

The moment we experience a second of (perceived) boredom, on goes the TV or we pick up our phone and start scrolling socials. We have stopped valuing stillness. In fact, many of us feel guilty when we do nothing. We look at the dishes in the sink, the emails that have not been responded to, or the likes and comments that have gone unacknowledged.

It's all *go go go! Faster faster faster! More more more!*

Taking time out to stop and do nothing allows space for our brains to wind back and access the parts that boost creativity. The term 'monkey brain' refers to a mind that constantly jumps from one distraction to another. Presented with a problem, the monkey brain leaps straight to the most obvious answer. When we give ourselves the time to go beyond the obvious, we are able to access more creative, breakthrough, inventive and, dare I say, life-changing ideas.

Kieran Flanagan is, among other things, a speaker, author and thought leader in the area of creative problem solving and critical thinking. One of my favourite quotes from her is this: 'Too often we fall in love with our second idea.'

Faced with a problem, our search for a solution is often too narrow. We may consider just three options. We dismiss our first 'rubbish' idea in favour of a second, try a third, 'usually also rubbish', before settling on the second.

Her process is to take a piece of A4 paper and fold it in half four times to create 16 'boxes'. She writes an idea in each box, which gives her 16 ideas to work with before settling on the final solution. In fact, she has been known to generate 10 pages before a meeting, providing 160 ideas!

Creating the space to think gives us access to more.

The irony is that if we are to be more productive, to come up with good ideas and reach good decisions, we need to slow down and do less.

We also need to reframe boredom. We might think of it not only as an opportunity to pause but as a call to action.

Boredom lets you know when something is wrong. When you are constantly on the go, getting stuff done and ticking off items on those lists, you may ignore emotions that need to be attended to or miss what your inner voice is saying. Better to deal with emotions than become a slave to them.

I had a friend who would never allow herself to stop because she didn't like what her brain said to her when she did. Ultimately it led to a breakdown and a diagnosis of clinical depression—and a long, enforced break to work on her 'stuff'.

Doing nothing also makes us kinder. When we allow our thoughts to drift to a larger sense of purpose, we begin to think about meaningful activities that extend beyond our own lives. If we reframe boredom from 'not being productive' to 'investing in my wellbeing', we recognise it is as important as any other wellbeing activities we undertake, like exercising or thinking about nutrition.

In 2017 I travelled to New York with a couple of colleagues—well, they are mates, really—for a conference. Despite the fact we had only three days, we chose to spend one whole afternoon lying on the grass in the middle of Central Park. For me, it was the highlight of the trip.

This brings me to the tradition of *shinrin-yoku*, or forest bathing, a national pastime in Japan that's believed to reduce stress and promote wellbeing. It isn't about hiking or other physical exercise; it is simply being in nature, perhaps lying down on the forest floor and looking up at the treetops and the clouds. When we do this, we let the alpha brainwaves, responsible for creativity, out for a stroll. Studies indicate that a two-hour forest bath has real health benefits beyond simply slowing down, destressing and relaxing.

But it goes beyond just stopping and hanging out with trees. When was the last time you stopped and took some lung-filling, diaphragm-lowering deep breaths?

When we feel we have lost control, one way we can take it back immediately is to stop and take deep breaths.

Recent studies have shown that while quick, shallow and unfocused breathing may contribute to a host of problems, including anxiety, depression and high blood pressure, having greater control over our lungs can bring many benefits to our mental and physical health. In fact, scientists report that a particular frequency of breath — around six exhalations a minute — can be especially restorative, triggering a 'relaxation response' in the brain and body.

Of course, these findings are not new. Any practitioner of meditation or yoga knows that it's all in the breathing.

This goes beyond mindfulness, which tends to involve passive observation, like 'watching the breath'. To really benefit you need to do 'breath work' to actively change the way you breathe. This might involve consciously breathing more slowly and with your diaphragm (rather than the movement of your chest), so you can draw more air into your lungs.

Richie Bostock, 'the breath guy', explains in his book *Exhale* that slow, deep breaths set off a domino effect of physiological responses that speed up your fall into a more complete state of relaxation.

So take a deep breath and remind yourself that you are the boss of you, and that you are in control!

Decompress

Often our feelings of being out of control result from our having so much going on that we can't keep up. As we discovered in Experiment 1, writing things down is the best way to start to feel under control and reduce the sense of being mentally overwhelmed.

But our to-do lists keep getting longer. Even if you are quite well organised, I bet you move things from today's list to the next day's, then the next, and then the next. We have about a hundred different things on our minds at any given moment. In fact, a new study by psychologists at Queen's University in Kingston, Ontario, suggests that an average person has 6200 thoughts per day. That's a lot of thoughts!

Simply thinking about all the things we have going on is enough to make us feel stressed—and, in turn, cause us to be unproductive.

We become so crippled by thinking about all the things we need to do that we resort to doing all the wrong things, so we end up feeling unfulfilled at the end of the day. Sadly, we often repeat the cycle day after day.

Fortunately, one effective first-step exercise to resolve this issue is to write things down.

It's a simple and very powerful way to record anything and everything that requires your attention—client meetings, shopping lists, a 'big idea' you thought of in the car, a business strategy, the new habit you're trying to acquire, that quote you liked, your sister's birthday—so you have ready access to them.

It's a bit like a computer. Imagine how overwhelming it would be if every time you opened your computer every single file opened on your desktop! There's a good reason that we file them away in folders.

Productivity consultant David Allen reminds us in his book *Getting Things Done: The Art of Stress-Free Productivity*, 'Our minds are for having ideas, not storing them!'

Take a moment and list everything you have in your mind right now. Go ahead. I'll wait. Write down everything from 'replace batteries in smoke detectors' to 'research next holiday' to 'prepare client presentation' to 'empty dishwasher' and 'put a load of washing on'.

As trivial as it may seem, list-making has significant and proven benefits for turning chaos into order. Writing things down produces a sense of relief. It's like a weight being lifted from your shoulders. It doesn't matter if you haven't done all the things on your list; downloading onto paper in itself creates a sense of relaxation.

Still need convincing? Richard Branson, Tim Ferriss, Marie Forleo and Oprah (to name a few) are all fans of writing stuff down. Aristotle Onassis advised, 'Always carry a notebook. Write everything down ... That is a million-dollar lesson they don't teach you in business school!'

Decide

Having your goals, priorities and intentions in front of you in writing allows you literally to see and evaluate them:

» Which do you connect with the most?

» Which are imprecise and need fine-tuning?

» Which one should you do first?

» Which can be scheduled for later?

Even the most motivated folks occasionally sink into a place of self-doubt and hesitation. Keeping your goals list as a visible and constant reminder will help you maintain your resolve and remind you of your purpose. List them in your phone, stick them on the fridge, tape them to your mirror, jot them down in your diary.

When your brain isn't busy trying to retain everything, it is able to process anything. When you're not swamped you have the mental capacity to analyse and ask important questions:

» Given all the things I need to do, which one will have the biggest impact?

» Which 20 per cent of my activities yields 80 per cent of my results? (We'll return to the Pareto principle later.)

» Which activities can I eliminate, automate or delegate?

Sometimes it's the things we *don't* do that have the greatest impact.

Now we have stopped and taken stock of where we are at, we need to decide what to do next. In my experience many people approach this the wrong way around. They make decisions without understanding their current situation, capacity and commitments.

It's a bit like going shopping without checking what you already have in the pantry. You don't want to double up, but you don't want to run short either.

Before we dive into what it takes to make good decisions, let's consider for a minute one big potential decision. What are you *not* going to do?

When it comes to problem solving, we tend to add things rather than take them away. More on this in chapter 6, but in the meantime the first question you should ask yourself as you prioritise is 'Me or not me?'

When people approach me for help with productivity, typically they ask, 'How can I be more productive?' or, 'How can I find more time in my day?' As I've been arguing, the answer is not about *more*; it's about *less*. Figuring out what you are *not* going to do, or what you can take away, is the key to finding more space to think.

To help you choose, you need to understand decisions and how to make good ones. Decision making is the process we use to identify and choose between alternatives, recognising that a final choice may or may not result in an action.

It's basically a problem-solving activity. Medical Research Council researchers in the UK found that several structures within the brain are involved. These are the anterior cingulate cortex, the orbitofrontal cortex and the ventromedial prefrontal cortex.

You don't need to remember these names (I won't be testing you). What's interesting is how they behave. The brains of participants in the study showed different patterns of activity depending on whether they were told what to do or could freely decide.

When it comes to decision making, our brain doesn't react in the same way if we're following directions from someone else. It seems we prefer to be free to choose.

Another important aspect of the neuroscience of decision making is emotions. Many of us believe we make decisions based on rational choices, but the research suggests otherwise. For example, a study published in the journal *Cognition and Emotion* by social psychologists Jennifer Lerner and Dacher Keltner found that 'fearful people made pessimistic judgements of future events whereas angry people made optimistic judgements'.

In other words, when we are not in full control of our emotions, we are at risk of making dumb decisions.

There are many reasons why smart people make poor decisions.

For example, information overload may result in an illusion of knowledge, which can result in analysis paralysis. We may base a decision on incomplete information, or we may rush into a poor decision when confronted by urgent deadlines. If we lack the necessary emotional or physical resources—if we are too tired or stressed to think clearly—we will make poor decisions. Lack of sleep has a tremendous impact on good decision making.

Thinking clearly and logically takes time. Studies show that people are more likely to make risky choices under time pressure. Faced with an important decision, we need to be sure we have time to consider all possibilities.

We can't talk about decision making without also mentioning decision fatigue, which comes about because of lack of thinking space. It's a vicious cycle really. To make good decisions, you need space to think, but to ensure you have that thinking space you need to make some better decisions!

Ever noticed that as the day wears on, your fuse gets shorter and your patience wears thin in meetings or discussions?

At 3 pm, when you've been asked to decide between option A or option B—something that could cost the company millions if you're wrong—you've probably sighed and said something like, 'Let's just go with option A and move on'.

When you leave important decisions until the afternoon, your cognitive alertness is impaired and you're more likely to be reactive—'You should be able to make that choice yourself!'—because you're overtired.

What applies at work also applies at home. My friend Roslyn says the one thing that drives her nuts as a working parent is that when she gets home from work, the first question she's asked is, 'What's for dinner?'

Decision fatigue also shows up as willpower. As the day goes on, and we begin to burn through our decision capacity, things we had planned to do (go to the gym, take the dog for a walk, hang out with the kids) suddenly feel too hard and we lack the impetus to do them.

What I know from the experience of writing *The First 2 Hours* is that we tend to do our best thinking in the morning. We need to stop at the end of the day and decompress. Write down everything that didn't get done (do a brain dump), and leave any important decisions for the following morning.

In the end, there are the things you need to do (responsibilities) and things you want to do (goals).

We cover more of this in chapter 5, when we talk about letting go of what is not serving our goals, and building a life by design.

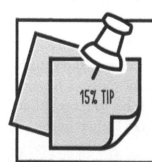

15% TIP

Go to your diary right now and block out the first two hours to be set aside for you. Protect that time to stop, breathe and get your pre-frontal cortex back in control.

Weighty decisions

My friend Brian is a shift worker. He has always found it challenging to keep aspects of his life under control, particularly his health. Following the *decelerate, decompress and decide* framework, he was able to make significant improvements to his health that had a knock-on effect in other aspects of his life.

He had been told he was pre-diabetic and had stopped running, something he had loved doing in the past. Within six months of taking time out for himself (decelerating), assessing what he needed to do (decompressing) and putting his health first (deciding), he had shed 30 kg, was running again, and had his blood tests back within the normal range.

CONDUCT AN
EXPERIMENT

EXPERIMENT 4

Time to Kanban your to-do list!

What's Kanban? you ask (see figure 4.2). A Kanban board visually depicts work or tasks at various stages of progress towards completion using cards (or sticky notes). It has its roots in lean manufacturing, and for our purposes we can keep it simple.

I prefer the old-fashioned sticky note on a wall or whiteboard, but there are plenty of great software options as well. I'll leave you to decide what you prefer.

To do (or backlog)	In progress	Completed

Figure 4.2: Kanban

Put all the individual tasks or items on sticky notes. (Initially they will all be in the first column.) Choose no more than five (three is best) from the first column to move to the second column. These are what you are working on today or this week. As you complete a task, move the sticky note to the third column, then choose another task from the first column to move into the second.

PAUSE FOR A MOMENT

How much time can you block out in your diary that you feel you will be able to protect, no matter what?

When someone asks you for that time, what will you say? Rehearse this so it rolls off the tongue and doesn't sound like a rejection.

What would it take to keep that time sacrosanct? What would you be sacrificing if you were to give up that time?

CHAPTER 5
Breathing space

My friend Anna is an inspiration. She is the best person I know at creating boundaries. My favourite thing she does, which everyone who works with her knows about, is stopping for tea at 3 pm. In fact, if she wrote a memoir, it would be called *Tea at 3*.

This simple act of stopping for a cup of tea at a designated time may seem trivial, but it's a great way to create some breathing space. In the 30 minutes she sips her tea and enjoys a sweet treat, she frees her mind from the worries of life. She sits back and enjoys the moment.

Her ability to block out the world and just *be* is something I have long admired. There have been times when I have gone to pick up the phone to call her, then noticed the time is 3.10 pm, say, and thought to myself, *No! I don't want to interrupt her tea at 3!*

Anna is very good at deciding how she wants to spend her time, and with whom.

Her father is in aged care, and she would not cancel her weekend visit to him for anything. She attends her local gym for Pilates and is strict about that, too. She will often say to me, 'I can't do that, I need to go to Pilates.' Her son plays basketball and soccer and she always makes time to attend his games. When I visit her (she lives interstate) she'll say, 'Just so you know, I am going to go to soccer at 10. You can come if you want.'

She manages all this at the same time as she holds down her position as associate partner at one of the big four financial services firms, where she is often described as cool under pressure, calm in the face of chaos and a safe pair of hands.

I may have given you the impression that she lacks flexibility. I would stress, rather, that she has created solid boundaries that serve her and the important people in her life.

Creating breathing space in our personal lives helps us focus and attend to the things that are important to us. It's a way of dealing with the problem of lack of capacity that means we may be failing at the important things in our lives.

Creating breathing space every day will help you get clear up front about what it is you want to achieve and then take action to ensure you achieve that goal.

Breathing space helps us to be intentional around what's important in our lives. This informs where we devote our precious resources. It helps us to disengage from people and activities that aren't bringing us joy and from things that prevent us from being our best selves.

Saying no or letting go can be one of the hardest things we will ever do. And it's one of the only ways we will be able to find that 15 per cent capacity for the important things.

Figure 5.1 (overleaf) shows what we need to do to let go and create breathing space:

1. **Disengage** from people, activities and things that are taking up our valuable time and space.

2. **Disconnect** from technology so we can reconnect with ourselves.

3. **Devote** time and energy to the things that are important to us.

Disengage

Disengaging is mostly about letting go of relationships and activities that take away oxygen. We find it difficult to let go of unfulfilling acquaintances, friends, relationships, jobs, partners ...

I read once that people come into your life for a reason, a season or a lifetime. And yet, once we have labelled someone 'friend', we automatically make it a lifetime engagement!

I have a few friendships that date back several decades, but I'm generally very good at recognising the reason and season folks. It may seem a bit cold, but we need to remember that as humans we constantly shed things, even people, we no longer need.

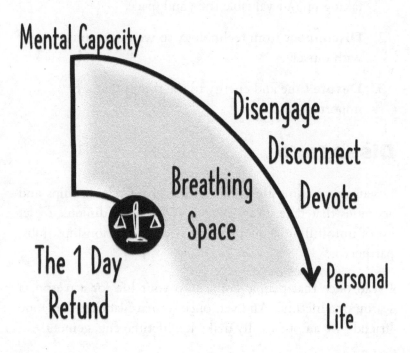

Figure 5.1: breathing space

When should we say farewell?

» When energy is sucked rather than shared or when the trade is inequitable. When you spend time with a friend, do you walk away energised, happy, inspired, informed? Or do you walk away feeling exhausted, depleted, drained?

» When priorities change. Milestones like getting married and having kids often trigger changes in longstanding relationships. You may start to see less of your single drinking buddies as you build relationships with others who are in a similar situation to you.

If you want to maintain relationships that are no longer the fit they once were, you need to set boundaries.

When people think of boundaries, many assume we are talking about rules that govern personal space. Healthy work-related boundaries go much deeper. They define how much of yourself you give to your career and guide how you form relationships with managers, colleagues and clients. They also help make time for the important things, like the people and activities in your life outside of work.

Personal boundaries set basic guidelines for the way you want to be treated, and ensure relationships are mutually respectful, appropriate and caring.

Healthy boundaries can mean the difference between career/work fulfilment and burnout.

They are the physical, emotional and mental limits you create to protect yourself from overcommitment, being used or unethical behaviour.

Remember the purple patches we talked about in chapter 4? A purple patch is a boundary, too. If we are going to create more capacity in our world by means of a refund, we will need more boundaries and we will need to make sure others know about them.

The good old 5 Ws are a great way to think about boundaries:

» **Who** am I willing, or not, to give time to?

» **What** do I want, or not want, to do or achieve?

» **When** do I need to protect time, and when do I want to make myself available?

» **Where** can I put in place contextual markers about the physical locations of work, play and rest?

» **Why** would I give one person or activity attention over another?

Creating boundaries around the pace at which we work means we are not going to be pushed into going flat out all the time. We will work more steadily.

Does this make you think of Aesop's fable of the tortoise and the hare? As you'll recall, the hare is so confident of winning a race with the tortoise that it stops part way to take a nap. The tortoise, for all that it proceeds very slowly, wins the race because it doesn't pause. It keeps its eyes on the prize and nothing distracts it!

The moral is that you will be more successful if you proceed slowly and steadily rather than quickly but erratically.

We learned in chapter 4 that when we act quickly and carelessly, we are probably responding to excess cortisol and adrenaline, and that this impairs clear thinking and good decision making.

Boundaries must therefore begin with us, and we must have the discipline to maintain them.

Think of boundaries as systems you put in place to ensure you work on the right things at the right time. The system outlined in the second book in this series, *The First 2 Hours*, explains how to erect boundaries based on time, for example.

As I have begun to suggest, one of the toughest acts of disengaging occurs when we realise we are in relationships that are not good for us. In my experience, ending a relationship with a toxic partner can be easier than ending a relationship with a toxic friend.

Many of us find ourselves trapped in what psychoanalyst Stephen Karpman terms the Drama Triangle. This model of social interaction comprises three archetypal dysfunctional personas trapped in a ceaseless cycle of conflict and role-switching, without resolution. We've all been there. You can probably name people in your family who take up these roles.

Can you identify yourself in this framework?

» **Persecutor:** 'It's all your fault!' The villain of the piece is controlling, oppressive, critical, superior and aggressive.

» **Victim:** 'Poor me!' The passive and persecuted underdog feels helpless and is unable to make decisions, solve problems or enjoy what life offers.

Victims unconsciously seek out persecutors and rescuers in order to absolve themselves of responsibility for failure. Rescuers may save the day, but in doing so they perpetuate the victim's sense of helplessness.

» **Rescuer:** 'Let me help you!' The classic hero-as-enabler feels guilty if they don't step in. Rescuers seek value in being needed by others, but their actions are often a way to avoid their own problems. Their interventions are often bandaids rather than sustainable solutions.

Let me put this into context. About ten years ago I had a victim in my life named Geoff (not his real name). His ex-wife (the persecutor), if you believed Geoff, stayed up nights coming up with new and interesting ways to make his life miserable.

Geoff would regularly come to visit and regale me (the rescuer) with stories of his ex-wife's latest antics. I would respond with words of support, encouragement and suggestions.

I always felt exhausted when he left. The thing about victims is that they are energy vampires who suck the life out of you. My husband would find me lying listlessly on the couch and ask, 'Has Geoff been here again?'

Then the phone would ring and Geoff would ask, 'Can I come over again tomorrow? You are sooooo motivating. I *love* hanging out with you.' And like a good little rescuer, I would always say, 'Yes, of course.'

I knew I had to break this cycle. I recognised my role as victim but felt helpless to escape.

It was then that I learned about personal growth educator David Emerald's Empowerment Dynamic (TED).

In this model, the Victim becomes the Creator. It might seem a stretch, but Emerald explains how those who have been in victim mode over a long period of time can get creative and consider their vision and goals. Creators are focused on outcomes, rather than on problems.

The Persecutor in this scenario takes on the role of Challenger, encouraging us to see obstacles as challenges that force us to clarify our goals or vision.

The Rescuer takes on the role of Coach. Instead of seeing it as their duty to rescue, a Coach asks questions intended to help the individual make informed choices. The key difference between a rescuer and a coach is that the coach enables the individual to make choices that allow them to solve their own problems. For the Rescuer, the Victim is broken. For the Coach, the client is creative, resourceful and whole.

I had a perfect opportunity to try out TED when Geoff visited with a new tale of persecution.

His ex-wife wanted to take their two children to Disneyland. She said it was so they could also visit her mother, who lives in southern California, for her birthday. Geoff knew better. It was really to prevent Geoff from having time with the kids in the school holidays. He told me he had already spoken with his lawyer and was planning to take out a court order preventing her from taking the children out of the country.

Now, normally, I would have responded with something like, 'Go, buddy!' or, 'What a great idea … here's what else you can do.' On this occasion, however, the empowerment dynamic was in my head and, refusing the role of Rescuer, I replied with what I thought was a great coaching question: 'What will the children think of that?'

I would love to tell you that Geoff replied, 'What a great question. I hadn't thought of that', but the truth is he grabbed his backpack and stormed to the door. Through gritted teeth he said, 'I knew it! Eventually everyone is on her side.' I never saw him again.

Once I recovered from the shock, I reflected on what I had hoped to achieve from this interaction: to no longer have a Victim/Rescuer relationship with Geoff. So, in a manner of speaking, I was successful. I no longer had a Victim in my world.

Yet I really wanted to be a better Coach. What if this had been an important relationship I really wanted to maintain? What if the Victim had been, say, a family member? I realised that I should have paced our transitions to our new roles. I had done the verbal equivalent of throwing a bucket of iced water over his head. And here's why.

In the mind of a Victim there are only two kinds of people: Persecutors and Rescuers. So when I stepped away from the role of Rescuer, he immediately placed me in the role of Persecutor.

When Geoff said, 'I'm taking out a court order', I could have started with a series of more supportive comments:

» 'This is clearly important to you.'

» 'Court orders are expensive.'

» 'You have spent a lot of money with your lawyer this year.'

» 'Do the children know?' If not: 'How do you think they will feel when they find out?' If yes: 'How do you think they feel?'

Geoff might have chosen to remain in the role of Victim, but this pacing and leading would have increased my chances of maintaining the relationship.

Why did I tell you this story? Because I would bet a gazillion dollars that at least one of your current relationships has this dynamic. This is exactly the kind of relationship we need to remove or adjust so it doesn't take up all our energy and time.

Victims will take as much as you are willing to give, and until you disengage from them, or shift the dynamic, you will not be able to get the breathing space you need.

Disconnect

With all the distractions and competing priorities in our lives it's easy to become overwhelmed and lose focus on what's truly important.

Things like your health, family and friends often take a back seat when, in fact, they bring us more energy and inspiration.

Connecting to your higher purpose gives you a reason for doing what you do. It's the key to motivation. Being connected to purpose and your inner self increases your productivity and will create more capacity along with a strong sense of balance and achievement. For this to happen, we need ways to disconnect and reconnect. Unplugging from socials and email for just 10 minutes, for example, will give your brain an opportunity to organise your thoughts.

More than 3000 medical studies have shown the positive impact of meditation, and all power to you if you already practise it. There's no doubt you will reap the benefits these studies have identified. Sometimes I find the simple act of sitting and relaxing can be enough to quiet my brain, helping me to catalogue thoughts, information or ideas while my mind is still.

Lynne Cazaly, facilitator and author of a number of valuable books including *Ish* and *Argh!*, reminds us we need time to *detach* from all the inputs our brains are subject to. She recommends that after a long and perhaps tedious meeting, online or face-to-face, you take a quick break while you connect to something unrelated to work. For example, if you are at home, grab a broom and sweep the deck, or take a long leisurely time to make tea or coffee. Allow your mind to relax and unload while the cuppa is brewing.

When I lived in China, my desk neighbour would stop at 2 pm every day, ceremoniously take a piece of fruit out of her bag, look at it (somewhat lovingly) and wander off to the kitchen. After several days of watching this ritual, I followed her and asked about it.

I discovered it was a deliberate, purposeful activity: 'When I stop and take the time to prepare the fruit, sit down and enjoy eating each mouthful, I have a chance to have a break.

It's not only healthy because of eating the fruit, but it gives me a full 15-minute break, which fuels my ability to work through until the end of the day.'

When you are not deliberate as my colleague was, you may waste time on unimportant activities and be more easily distracted.

Each day, write down the three important activities you want to achieve so your intentional commitment is communicated to your brain. It won't take long for others to see where your focus lies.

Only some activities, relationships, teamwork and collaboration will help you achieve the result you want, which means you need to focus on maximising those and saying no to everything else. This helps to create stronger boundaries that will help you be more present in terms of where, on what, and with whom you spend your time.

The second of Stephen Covey's 7 *Habits of Highly Effective People* is to 'begin with the end in mind'. It describes making a conscious effort to imagine what you want in life. In defining your personal, moral and ethical guidelines, you lay the groundwork for becoming a happy and fulfilled person. Beyond a task list, it's about truly defining the personal environment you want to inhabit.

Once this is clear, boundaries, decisions and the letting go of things like toxic relationships becomes easier.

Time is too precious a commodity to waste on things that aren't bringing us what we want. Don't wait until it's too late!

Devote

Bronnie Ware is an Australian author who spent several years nursing in palliative care with patients in the last 12 weeks of their lives. She recorded their dying epiphanies in a blog called *Inspiration and Chai*, which got so much attention she gathered her observations into a book called *The Top Five Regrets of the Dying*:

1. I wish I'd had the courage to live a life true to myself rather than the life others expected of me.

2. I wish I hadn't worked so hard.

3. I wish I'd had the courage to express my feelings.

4. I wish I had stayed in touch with my friends.

5. I wish I had let myself be happier.

So where do you think you should be devoting more time? And where do you need 15 per cent breathing space so you can be true, stay in touch and let yourself be happier?

Frankly, this should be the end game. Why am I giving myself a refund to achieve more capacity if not to do things that fill me with joy?

It may seem weird to be writing about joy or happiness when it comes to productivity, but there are some very real benefits in making sure we are living joyful lives. Studies going back to 2005 show that joyful people are less likely to suffer heart attacks. They maintain healthier blood pressure and tend to have lower cholesterol levels.

Research also suggests joy boosts our immune systems, fights stress and pain, and improves our chances of living longer lives. And joyful people tend to be more patient, kind and creative than their peers. Studies indicate that they're also more likely to have healthy, meaningful relationships that last.

I often hear people say they are too busy to engage in joyful pursuits. They are focused on their work or career. That would make sense if not for the research that shows that joyful people are 40 per cent more likely to be promoted at work.

Research conducted by three economists who work in the area of human wellbeing, Jan-Emmanuel De Neve, George Ward and Clement Bellet, found that when workers are happier, they work faster and more productively. In the case of call-centre workers, they make more calls and convert more calls to sales.

More importantly for the purpose of this book, they found that happy workers do not work more hours than less contented colleagues—they are simply more productive.

The verdict is in! We know from the work of neuroscientists that our brains work better when they are in a positive state, as opposed to a negative, neutral or stressed state, so prioritising your joy could be the magic ingredient for your productivity success.

Martin Seligman, the father of positive psychology, identifies three types of happy lives:

» **The pleasant life.** Having pleasant experiences like falling in love, taking holidays, attending parties. He recommends things like learning, savouring and mindfulness—techniques that amplify these experiences.

» **The life of engagement.** Being in touch with your inner self and strengths. Knowing your strengths and creating a life that enables you to use them provides a greater sense of fulfilment.

» **The meaningful life.** Like the life of engagement, it involves using your strengths in the service of something larger than yourself.

Seligman's research also shows that, in general, optimists try harder, as they believe their efforts will make a difference and are often willing to give something a go even when the odds are stacked against them. It goes without saying that they get more done in less time than pessimists do.

And it's not just about devoting time to activities and others. It's also about how much time you protect to devote to yourself.

Carving out even 10 minutes a day can create breathing space. During periods of lockdown in Australia during 2020 and 2021, it was not always the people who were alone who struggled most. I had a number of conversations with (mostly) women who said they missed their privacy when every family member was forced to stay home all day. They had underestimated the time they used to have to themselves, however brief, after family members left the house for the day, or just before they came home, or when they were engaged in weekend activities.

My friend Angela said she would 'hide' in the toilet just to have 10 minutes when she couldn't be asked a question or be required to solve a problem or be the rock of support for others.

You shouldn't have to hide in the bathroom to make time for yourself!

Find some time to devote to yourself first, then to the other things that are important to you.

Deep diaphragmatic breathing helps lower the feelings of stress or anxiety that can, in turn, get in the way of your best work. Any time you are feeling overwhelmed, stop and breathe. Your future self will thank you.

Tech Shabbat

Tiffany Shlain built her career online. She is the founder of the Webby Awards, which honour the best of the Web each year. She also runs a film studio and creates online conversations.

Yet every Friday evening for over a decade Shlain and her family have unplugged their devices and spent the next 24 hours offline in what she calls a Technology Shabbat.

Tech Shabbat is a modern twist on an ancient Judaic religious practice that can benefit people of faith and nonbelievers equally.

(continued)

Shabbat is the day of the week reserved for rest and worship in Judaism. The Christian Sabbath has its origins in, and obviously takes its name from, Shabbat. Jews observe Shabbat on Saturdays, beginning Friday nights with lit candles and shared meals. In addition to resting from day-to-day work, Orthodox Jews also refrain from a number of other activities that once involved work, such as driving a car or switching on a light.

Seventh Day Adventists also take the Sabbath seriously, worshipping, avoiding work and spending time with other church members on Saturdays.

Most Christians worship on Sunday, though their observance of a day of rest varies from church to church and from individual to individual.

Even if it's not about religious observance for you, the simple ritual of disconnecting at 5 pm on Fridays for 24 hours might be enough to give you the space to spend time with people or on activities that bring you joy.

A Tech Sabbath can take lots of different shapes, but what's important is that, however briefly, we consciously step out of our everyday life in order to reflect.

It makes a lot of sense for anyone who is looking at the health benefits of unplugging from the world of devices.

A growing body of psychological and neuroscientific research suggests that constantly staring at screens may be making us more 'distracted, distant and drained' and that rapid clicking from screen to screen is making it more difficult for us to engage deeply. Studies of social media use link screen time to such problems as loneliness and disrupted sleep.

EXPERIMENT 5

For the next 30 days, set a timer on your watch for a specific time — let's say 10 am — take three deep breaths, and write down three things in that moment for which you are grateful.

Don't worry if what you write is repetitious; you are allowed be grateful every day for having a job you love!

PAUSE FOR A MOMENT

Think of three things that nourish you or bring you joy. Keep adding to this list. These are things, large and small, you can do regularly in your life to cultivate joy.

What are you grateful for? Keep a gratitude journal and periodically record up to five things for which you're grateful.

What could you do to acknowledge your gratitude for your life? It could be anything from helping others, smiling at a stranger on the street or sending a thank you card to a friend to volunteering in your community. There are so many ways we can help each other every day. It is not how much we give, but how much love we put into the giving.

CHAPTER 6
Living space

Marie Kondo has made a significant pile of money from helping people improve their living spaces. But even if you were the most devoted fan of her method, I'm not sure you would have been prepared for what 2020 threw at us, with the need to work at home, supervise the kids' learning at home, relax and basically live at home, sometimes 100 per cent of the time!

We have all experienced overflowing wardrobes, double-stacked bookcases, a chaotic desk, bottomless catch-all drawers, and plasticware cupboards from which containers (with missing lids) tumble every time we open them.

We've all stood in front of that overflowing wardrobe and cried, 'I don't have a thing to wear', when the evidence in front of us shows the opposite is true. We have too much to wear!

Every one of these examples stops us from operating effectively, slowing us down because we can never find things when we need them.

Creating just 15 per cent extra physical space can improve our productivity!

Creating more physical space in our world is about removing friction, about creating a world in which there's a place for everything and everything goes back into its place. I know this sounds like a cliché on a cross-stitch sampler made by your nanna, but the advice is sound.

James, a travel agent, told me that one of the things that created the most friction for him at work was pens. He could never find one. This was because colleagues would borrow a pen and not give it back and clients would use his pen to sign documents then absent-mindedly pocket it. Rather than fight a losing battle, at the end of every day James would sticky-tape three pens to the underside of his desk so he could always put his hand on a pen when he needed it.

Rather than getting grumpy at co-workers or clients, he came up with a simple solution that had a significant impact on his wellbeing … and his relationships!

Figure 6.1 shows us the three things we need to focus on to free up and create more living space:

1. **Design**. Think about the kind of space you want to live in and the practical elements needed to create it.

2. **Declutter**. Create a living space in which there is literally room to move around.

3. **Decomplicate**. Reduce the number of steps, or complications, required to get something done.

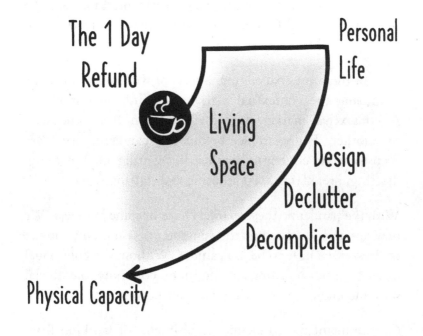

Figure 6.1: living space

Design

Whether you are working from home or from an office, it's important to design your space for better living and productivity.

As a result of the COVID-19 pandemic we have experienced overlaps across multiple areas of our lives. One thing I found particularly difficult initially was clearly marking out the space between work, home, relaxation, play and times when I really needed to concentrate.

One of the most challenging aspects of working from home is missing the contextual markers that inform our habits. A contextual marker flags the transition from one state to another. For example, before the pandemic we were accustomed to contextual markers like getting up, showering, dressing, breakfasting, commuting and starting work.

With the pandemic these markers have become less clear. We may get up and switch on the computer first and only shower or dress if we have to be 'on camera'. Without the contextual markers of our morning and afternoon commute, the official start and end of the working day have become blurred.

One result of the pandemic 'experiment' of working from home is that in future more of those of us who can, will choose to work from home for at least part of the working week. Designing and physically marking out space at home has, as a result, become increasingly important.

Having a dedicated workspace at home has many benefits. The smallest of spaces, even a one-room bedsit, can be adapted effectively.

A dedicated space allows you to focus, to get into work mode mentally. It minimises distractions and helps you create a work–life balance while working from home.

Here are some more tips.

MAKE A SPACE

This may seem like the easy one, but it's important to give it some thought. A spare room makes things a little easier—it will give you some privacy, and you can shut the door on it when you stop work!

In smaller spaces, however, this is not always an option. Setting up a workstation in your dining room/kitchen may be your only option. The lighting in these areas is usually pretty good and you can probably access ample counter space.

If possible, create a workstation that has natural light, allows for privacy to make calls, and doesn't conflict with the activities of other members of your household.

MAKE IT TIDY

I think it's fascinating how little we have learned to live with when it comes to work. Remember the old days when we had drawers, cabinets, magazine boxes full of paper and important documents? Now it's easy to keep our workstation/desk clear, organised and portable, with a laptop and, if necessary, a notebook.

If your workspace has to be in a shared space like a kitchen bench or table, make sure you pack your work away at the end of the workday. Otherwise, it may get damaged—and you may be tempted to keep working. Decluttering at the end of the day ensures you start your next workday with a clean slate.

MAKE IT HOSPITABLE

Set up a space that you *want* to work in. One of the benefits of working from home is you are free to create an area that helps you thrive and be productive. Add a plant, hang a picture, set up an adjustable light and pop a cushion nearby for the family pooch!

Don't overlook the benefits of moving the workstation to the veranda, backyard or balcony when the weather is nice.

MAKE IT COMFORTABLE

If you are going to invest in one thing, make it a chair. If you are sitting for long periods, you'll want to save your back! Many people either purchase or jerry-rig standing desks, with obvious mental and physical health benefits.

MAKE IT SEPARATE

Working from home can make the transition to home time difficult. Many of us can't avoid the temptation of the computer that's right there.

Having a dedicated workspace helps. When you finish for the day, close the lid and put your computer out of temptation's way. Being able to separate your work and home environments visually acts as a cue to your brain (and to those you live with) that you are not working.

If you are wondering whether the design principles I've outlined would work in your home, and not only as a working-from-home consideration, remember that domestic spaces are already designed with storage, hospitality, comfort and separation in mind.

Most homes are marked out or designed according to function. For example, most have spaces for cooking and eating, relaxing and watching TV, sleeping, showering and so on. Problems arise when these spaces become blurred because stuff overflows from one space to another.

I confess I'm a bit of a fan of IKEA. Not so much their disposable furniture but their cool storage and organisation products. It's easy to design a tidy pantry, linen closet or underwear drawer if you have the right containers and dividers. It almost becomes a pride thing!

Declutter

Clutter creates physical and mental obstructions and dis-tractions. If you work from home, it's tough to stay organised and on task when piles of stuff impinge on your workspace.

When you are surrounded by too many things, you may feel pressured to clean up. Or you'll feel guilty about the mess. We have all experienced the satisfaction of taking a little time out to tidy up. Sometimes this may be an excuse to procrastinate, but the research suggests we get more done in a tidy space. You'll also free up more thinking space in your brain because you won't have so many visual distractions that prompt guilt, anxiety and stress.

In early 2021 I sold my house in regional Victoria and moved to the better climate of South East Queensland. We downsized considerably and faced the prospect of squeezing the contents of a large farmhouse into a narrow townhouse. Because we had to get rid of so much stuff, for a time we had a skip parked outside almost permanently. It reminded me that often we declutter only when we have a reason to—like moving to a new home or the imminent arrival of guests that prompts organising that spare room.

This has happened to me at work too, when moving offices necessitates decisions about the clutter we have accumulated over several years at the same workstation.

I've made it my business to declutter monthly at work, and quarterly at home. There's something cathartic about getting rid of things.

If you are not sure about what to get rid of, here are 10 suggestions to get you started:

» Take-away menus: Seriously we just don't need them anymore.

» Cardboard boxes: I'm hopeless with these. I tend to keep the boxes technology comes in, just in case. Not anymore! Straight into the recycling bin for you!

» Extra water bottles: You only need one, maybe two if you want one permanently in the car.

» Souvenir t-shirts: You know, from that 5K run you did years ago, or marking any other occasion. At the time it seemed like a good memento, but you wouldn't wear it in public now.

» Decades-old Christmas or birthday cards: What are you even keeping these for?

» Supplies from your defunct hobby: Time to let it go. If you haven't picked it up in three years, chances are you won't ever again.

» Books you've read: Eek! That's a tough one! By all means, keep the classics you love or those that are especially meaningful to you, but I think it's okay to let go of your collection of Jeffrey Archer or John Grisham books. No judgement!

» Old makeup and nail polish: They're all there in that drawer in the bathroom you never open.

» Useless swag: I've stopped bringing stuff home from conferences and I've also stopped giving it. I don't need another water bottle (see earlier point) or plastic carry bag, or branded notepad and pen.

» Incomplete games and jigsaws: Any game that is missing a piece is just taking up space in your cupboard. And that 1000-piece jigsaw is unlikely to see the light of day again once it's been done. Let it go to a new home to challenge someone else.

The real trick is trying not to bring new stuff home.

My niece has three children under three, thanks to a set of twins. She has asked the family to stop buying stuff for her kids. It's not that she's mean or an ingrate; it's just that they have *so much stuff*. She also only ever buys second-hand toys and kiddie equipment for birthdays and Christmas. She is all about recycling and upcycling as a way to help protect the planet.

I know that we are in the personal life section of the book, but if you have a cluttered workspace, you will not do your best work. Some people claim they can work in 'organised chaos', but the research suggests it's simply not true.

Studies show that a cluttered workspace is the enemy of productivity and decision making. Further, people whose workspaces are tidy are kinder, more generous and more likely to make healthy eating choices than those in disorganised spaces.

Mess is distracting. Too much in your field of vision makes it difficult to keep your attention on the one thing you need to focus on.

Here are a few things you can do to declutter your workspace:

» **Start small.** Choose one area—maybe a desk drawer or single stack of papers—and focus on that.

» **Box it up.** Remove everything from your desk aside from your laptop and phone (and any other absolute essentials) and put it all in a box. You can bring stuff back as you find you need it, but the rest remains boxed. After a while you may find you can simply toss the box!

» **Stop printing.** Saving to the cloud means we shouldn't need printouts anymore. They just take up space.

» **Tidy up your cables.** Most of us live with a tangled mess of power cables around our workspaces. Grab some cable ties or clips and run them neatly together, and put phone chargers, headphones and adapters away when you are not using them.

When it comes to digital clutter, don't forget to:

» tidy up your computer desktop

» archive emails and files (anything older than 12 months)

» turn off notifications (including the little red circle indicators on your smartphone).

If you're concerned about mental clutter, refer back to chapter 2. Also:

» **Keep a journal.** Writing down your thoughts in a notebook, journal or planner is a great way of decluttering your mind. Research shows that having ideas or incomplete goals hovering about in our heads is distracting. Your chances of achieving them go through the roof when you write them down. It also helps clear away anxiety.

» **Keep a to-do list.** It happens to all of us. You are trying to focus on something, but you keep being distracted by thoughts of other things that need to be done. Jotting down these things as they come into your head will not only clear some capacity in there, but also increase the likelihood of your both remembering and completing said tasks.

Decomplicate

Decomplicating is about removing from tasks (or life) unnecessary steps or processes that repeatedly take extra time and energy.

Decomplicating is connected to decluttering. As the original time-management guru Benjamin Franklin famously put it, it comes down to 'a place for everything and everything in its place'.

What are the things at home you can never lay your hands on when you need them? For me it's:

» **car keys.** How elusive they are!

» **lip balm.** Despite buying them in packs every time I travel, I can never find one when my lips are feeling chapped.

» **tape measure.** For an item used so rarely, it creates a bunch of stress every time I can't find it.

» **reading glasses.** I always leave them in a 'safe place'!

» **scissors.** Somewhere there are at least 10 pairs—hiding in plain sight, no doubt!

» **screwdriver.** When I need a Phillips head, I find a flat head; when I need a flat head, I find a Phillips, always.

The remedy is to have a place for each of them, but the real kicker is to put them back there after using them. Your future self will thank you for taking that extra 30 seconds.

In addition to keeping things in their place, we need to think about how we can remove things to create a simpler, more streamlined life.

In 1940, Maurice and Richard McDonald opened a restaurant named McDonald's Bar-B-Que. Most of its 25 menu items were barbecued. Recognising that almost all of their profits came from selling hamburgers, in October 1948 the brothers established a streamlined system, setting up their kitchen like an assembly line to ensure maximum efficiency. They reduced the menu to a few main items, mostly hamburgers, and simplified the restaurant's name to McDonald's.

When the McDonald brothers streamlined their kitchens, they took a *heap* of stuff away to create space for the work and food to flow frictionlessly around a limited space.

Recent research indicates that when we're presented with a problem, our instinct is to 'add things' (complicate) rather than 'remove things' (decomplicate).

This instinct can be found everywhere. We set up extra meetings to figure out why work schedules are too cramped, but in doing so add more red tape, more decision points. One of my favourites from my old local area network (LAN) manager days is that when we are struggling for space in a computer network, we simply add more disk space.

Think about the way we learn to ride a bike. If you are like me, you probably started out with training wheels, and you taught your kids how to ride the same way. Turns out, that's not the most effective way to do it. The biggest obstacle for kids to overcome is how to balance and this is why the Strider, or balance bike, is so effective. By taking away the pedals, the child can practise balancing while keeping their feet near to the ground.

Now, I'm not entirely sure that the pedals and training wheels constitute 15 per cent of the bike, but you get the idea.

This idea is not new.

Leonardo da Vinci noted that perfection is achieved not when there is nothing more to add but when there is nothing left to take away. The Chinese philosopher Lao Tzu said, 'To attain knowledge, add things every day. To attain wisdom, subtract things every day.'

It seems we have been overcomplicating things for a very long time!

One of my personal favourite observations is much more recent. It was made by fashion designer and style icon Coco Chanel, who advised, 'Before you leave the house, look in the mirror and take one thing off.'

Here are some questions to ponder:

» Where could you decomplicate your systems, or reduce the number of things going on in your life, to make things feel more streamlined?

» When it comes to capacity, we can either build a bigger box, or take stuff out of the existing box. Which do you tend to do?

» When one wardrobe is full, do you overflow into another, or do you take a few bags to St Vinnie's?

» When you are tidying up, do you make a mercy dash to IKEA to buy more storage containers, or do you take a load of stuff to the dump?

» When your day or week is full, do you get up earlier or stay up later or do you reduce the number of things you commit to?

When seeking to reduce obstacles to leading a more productive, decomplicated, frictionless life, there are many ways we can take away rather than add things.

One of the most effective is reducing the number of decisions you have to make. Decision fatigue is a well-documented phenomenon. Simply put, it is the deterioration of our ability to make good decisions after a long period of decision making. In other words, the more decisions you need to make, the worse you're going to be at weighing all the options and making an educated, research-backed choice.

Reducing the number of decisions you make in a day can help you get your 15 per cent refund:

» Decide before you go to bed what you will wear tomorrow, or wear the same thing every day, as Steve Jobs did!

» Plan meals for the week, or even outsource meal planning (think Hello Fresh).

» Delegate decision-making authority to others.

» Block time in your day for specific things, so you aren't at the mercy either of email demands or other people's decisions.

» Set reminders.

» Create checklists and routines.

Create living space that gives you the room to move around your life effortlessly and without friction. This is not to say that things won't still go wrong from time to time, or that unexpected things won't crop up.

This extra capacity will enable you to respond in a calm and stress-free way. Sounds good, doesn't it?

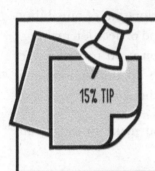

15% TIP

When packing stuff into boxes for storage, put a date on the outside indicating when you packed it. That way you know how long it's been since the box was opened, which may indicate whether or not you need to keep the contents.

Life changer

It took a pretty significant event for Liz to realise she wasn't really living; she was just existing. Caught up in the whirlwind of a chaotic life, she was chasing after an ideal career that wasn't only unrealistic but made her unhappy.

When she first came to me, she was literally out of breath from running. She had come from a series of back-to-back meetings that had already made her late, and because she couldn't find a closer parking spot, she'd had to park miles away in an expensive parking station and leg it to the café we were meeting at.

But I want to talk about our fourth meeting. We hadn't met for about three months, as she had experienced a personal tragedy she needed to deal with. During our earlier sessions, we had talked about needing to create more breathing and living space in her world, but she was always 'too busy' to make it happen.

When she sat down in front of me this time, it was like I was looking at a new person! She told me that the enforced stop had given her to an opportunity to take stock across a range of aspects of her life. She had made some decisions: to end relationships that no longer served her; to reconnect with people and things she had reluctantly let go; and to be very clear about where and how she wanted to spend her time.

'Time has become so precious to me and there's no way I'm wasting a second of it on anything that doesn't bring me joy and meaning.'

Not only that, she had done a massive clean-out of her home. She'd just had too much stuff, and junk that had accumulated over years. Moving it out was 'very cathartic'!

EXPERIMENT 6

My sister belongs to an online group that calls itself '40 bags in 40 days'. The idea is that each day, for 40 days, you take a bag of stuff out of your house. The size of the bag is up to you and in some cases it's symbolic. For you, it could be:

» a small shopping/grocery bag

» a large garbage bag

» a small zip-lock bag

» or even a suitcase full of emotional baggage (ha!).

The rule is that it has to actually be removed from the house, whether to be dropped into the garbage or recycling bin, or into the car to be donated, or to be listed on Gumtree.

If you don't know where to start, the pantry is a great place. Anything that's past its use-by date goes into the bag!

There are online groups advocating 'Buy nothing new for a month' and 'Shop your wardrobe for a year'. The first challenges you not to buy new clothing for a year, and the second shows you how to 'buy from your own stock'.

Challenge accepted!

PAUSE FOR A MOMENT

How could I declutter the space I'm working in right now?

How could I better design this space for greater productivity?

What could I take away, or stop doing, to create less friction and more flow?

CHAPTER 7
Working space

My daughter told me recently that she wished she could have one extra day a week. She is a happy, healthy woman who has a full and enjoyable life, but she is exhausted by the end of the week. She needs a one-day refund!

She is like many of us. When constantly juggling family, jobs, education, exercising and socialising, we simply run out of time. I'm sure you've felt it. At four on a Sunday afternoon you feel like your weekend is just starting!

You will know you are suffering from overload if:

» you love it when a scheduled appointment is cancelled because it gives you free time (a purple patch)

» you frequently say things like 'I'm too busy' or 'I don't have time'

» 75 per cent of your activities (like eating or driving) are done in tandem with others (like meetings, phone calls, scheduling)

» you feel obligated to respond immediately to emails, texts and phone calls, and find yourself judging others who don't do the same

» you feel you must check your phone and respond the second you receive a message or email

» you are over-scheduled, so you run from one thing to the next, and as a result you're often late

» you feel compelled to fill every waking moment with a productive activity (like checking emails while waiting in line at the bank).

I feel exhausted from just reading that list!

This chapter falls into the professional life part of our model, but some of the ideas here will also apply to your personal life. Let's face it, we have plenty of work or admin to do in our personal lives too, don't we? Your overloaded life probably encompasses:

» personal or life admin: renewing the car insurance, booking those flights, taking the dog to the vet

» work responsibilities: the full spectrum of tasks, from emails and fiddly jobs to people managing, troubleshooting, big-picture strategising and planning

» friends and family: helping your parents, your kids, your siblings and your friends with the challenges they're facing

» your relationship (if you're in one!): spending time with your partner, nurturing a fulfilling physical and emotional relationship, and making space for connection

» your physical self: exercising, healthy eating, playing hockey (in my daughter's case)

» and, although this one might feel like wishful thinking, your own spiritual and emotional wellbeing: going to concerts, galleries or exhibitions, being creative, travelling, exploring, being still, connecting to your spiritual side.

Now, I'm sure there's absolutely no need to convince you of just how much there is on your plate. You know this already. But if you're feeling there's too much to do and not enough time, the first half of that equation is one worth paying attention to. It could be that you are overcommitted and have trouble saying no. Reasons for this can include:

» unrealistic expectations

» constant noise

» absence of boundaries

» poor self-care

» running on empty

» perfectionism

» lack of self-awareness.

This is one of the quickest ways to recover space in your life. It comes from stripping away distractions, noise and activities that are not contributing to your life by design.

Creating the right working space gives us a line of sight on what we need to be doing. A life by design, as opposed to one by default.

Figure 7.1 shows us what we need to do to level up and create more working space:

1. **Define** and get clear about what we want.

2. **Defrag** our calendar and workdays.

3. **Delegate** to others.

Brené Brown puts it like this: 'Clarity is kind.' Being clear about your world is an act of kindness to yourself.

Define

Cricketer Sir Donald Bradman always dreamed of playing for Australia. As a young boy, he played long, solitary 'test matches' in which he took the part of every player of both the English and Australian sides.

He would spend countless hours every day throwing a golf ball at the base of a water tank with his right hand while holding a cricket stump in his left. The idea was that when the ball flew off the brickwork at an unpredictable angle, he would grip the stump with both hands and hit the ball before it could get past him and strike the laundry wall or door.

Such a feat is difficult at the best of times. The coordination of eye and arm was so precise that, as he said in a radio interview in 1988, even at the age of 9 or 10, he had learned to hit the golf ball with his stump 'more often than not'.

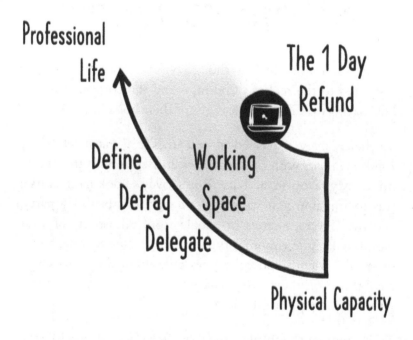

Figure 7.1: working space

At the Sydney Cricket Ground, during the summer of 1920–21, he watched Charlie Macartney making 170 and vowed to his father, 'I shall never be satisfied until I play on this ground.' In October 1926, a letter arrived from the New South Wales Cricket Association inviting him to attend practice at the SCG.

Defining is more than just setting goals. It's about having a vision for yourself, and all aspects of your life.

It can sometimes feel as though visions and missions are restricted to the realms of business and the corporate world, but maybe we can take a leaf out of their book.

Stephen Covey expressed it well in *The 7 Habits of Highly Effective People*, with habit number 2: 'Begin with the end in mind.' My favourite activity from Covey's book (and course) was to imagine you were at your eightieth birthday party, and there were a series of people from all aspects of your world making testimonial-type speeches. One by one, a mix of family, friends and colleagues talk about the impact you have made on their lives, what they remember you for and what they appreciate about you.

Take a moment to think about that. What would you like the most important people in your world to say about you? What legacy do you want to create?

If you have a personal vision, you are able to craft your future. In my experience it makes decisions easy. When you know where you are headed you can navigate effortlessly whatever challenges are thrown at you. Not only that, you know what to say 'no' to in order to maintain a maximum refund.

Your vision should guide your yearly, quarterly, monthly, weekly and daily activities.

It's okay to change your vision. In fact, you should review it every 5 or 10 years. Most organisations do this to ensure they are staying relevant, and I think it's equally useful for individuals.

Create a personal vision by answering any or all of the following questions:

» What will people say about you at your eightieth birthday celebration?

» How do you want to be remembered in your working life? What legacy would you be happy to create?

» What would you do if there were no restrictions and no boundaries?

» What would you do if you knew you couldn't fail?

» How would you spend your days if you won a gazillion dollars in a lottery?

Having a clear vision gives us capacity by reducing the need to take on things that don't move us towards our purpose or goals.

We can be crystal clear about what is the best use of our most valuable time. We will stop wasting time on things, people and activities that don't move us in the right direction. As a result, we will begin to create more capacity in our world.

Are you sure about it? I mean, are you really sure of what you want? For example, is your vision of being a real estate mogul with a portfolio of investment properties generating an income of approximately $250K a year really what you want? Are you prepared for the consequences?

Take a moment, right now, to think about your situation and answer these questions:

1. In relation to your vision, what is your current situation? Describe it fully by writing down what you are seeing, hearing and feeling.

2. Where do you want to be? What is your desired state? What do you want to achieve? Describe it fully by writing down what you want to see, hear and feel when you reach this state.

3. Why do you want to achieve this state? Start your answer with 'So that ...'

4. What is preventing you from reaching the desired state?

5. And what else? (Repeat this question as many times as necessary.

6. How will you know when you have reached your desired state?

7. If you could have it all *right now*, would you take it?

8. What would be the consequences of having your vision come to fruition?

Adjust your vision accordingly, then rinse and repeat this exercise until you feel in your bones that you have a clear definition of what you want to be, do and have.

Now you have defined what you want, it's time to create at least 15 per cent more space to attain it.

Defrag

For many of us, our workdays always feel insanely busy but are not always productive. You may not consider yourself a multitasker, but you may be a 'project jumper'.

Maybe you sit down to prepare a presentation, then answer a random email, then start writing a report before heading back to your inbox to respond to another message. You have no system that ensures you complete one job at a time. Instead, you jump from task to task in an effort to keep chipping away at your never-ending to-do list.

You may be constantly busy and reach the end of the day feeling exhausted, only to discover other large, looming projects still on your list. You have spent eight hours banging away on your computer but haven't actually completed anything of substance. Sound familiar?

To sort this out, you need to do a little micromanagement. There's no secret as to why Weight Watchers are the most successful weight-loss program ever! It's because their members focus on and attend to eating and exercising, counting every calorie they consume. They micromanage their food intake.

Keeping a detailed time sheet on where you are spending each hour works even better. You need only do it for 30 days to see opportunities for tightening up the way you use time. It will also show where you have fallen victim to the planning fallacy. This is the phenomenon by which predictions about how much time will be needed to complete a future task betray an optimism bias, underestimating the time needed.

I propose you micromanage where you spend your time so you can identify where your 15 per cent will come from.

One way you can do this is to defrag your day.

In a previous life, I was a LAN manager. I helped administer a digital network for about 40 users on 286 computers, which at the time were the latest and greatest. (I get it that I'm showing my age!) From time to time we would run a defrag process on the computers, particularly if they had started to run out of space or were running slow. Defragmentation or defragging is the process of reorganising the data stored on a hard drive so related pieces of data are put back together all lined up in a continuous fashion.

Figure 7.2 shows what it used to look like.

Instead of small chunks of data spread all over, it is compacted, leaving almost half the disk space available for use.

When you are looking to get your full refund, finding 30 minutes here and there won't work.

It would be like re-fragmenting your computer. We need to find ways to compress time, batch our work and create a good chunk of time (at least 90 minutes per day) as our refund. Let me remind you, this is not so you can goof off! It's so you can take a more proactive, relaxed and focused approach to your work.

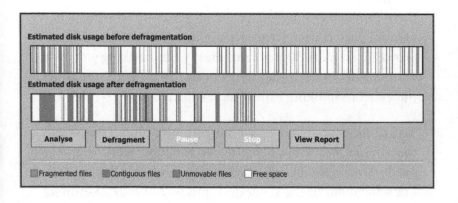

Figure 7.2: defragging

If you are serious about defragging your day, you will want to consider batching.

First, though, let's recall the evils of multitasking or project jumping.

Jenna Kutcher, blogger, social media expert and productivity coach, points out that the average time spent on a task before losing focus is just 1 minute and 15 seconds. We may think we are multitasking, but what we are really doing is switching our mind back and forth from one task to another. We are not giving either task our full attention. Multitaskers reduce their productivity by 40 per cent across the board. They take 50 per cent longer to accomplish a particular task, and errors increase by 50 per cent. Heavy multitasking can even temporarily lower IQ up to 15 points (which is three times the effect of smoking cannabis). It's the ultimate re-frag!

So I think we can agree on a 'no' to multitasking. But what's the alternative? Time blocking or batching work is a very productive and efficient way to get through piles of stuff. I'm a huge fan of the pomodoro method of four 25-minute bursts of work with five-minute breaks in between. It's how I have written all my books.

You could also use the Pareto principle, named for the Italian economist Vilfredo Pareto, to figure out how to make the best use of your most valuable time. According to this principle, 20 per cent of what you do gives you 80 per cent of your results!

Here's how you batch:

1. Make a list of everything you need to get done in your life. And when I say everything, I mean everything.

My own list includes all the tasks for my business and for my personal life. (See chapter 4 and the activities around decompressing.)

2. Group similar items together. For example, group personal or life admin together, or work-related tasks like preparing presentations, processing email (after lunch is best for this, as I explain in *The First 2 Hours*), budget reviews and forecasting.

3. Make a schedule and block the time required to complete each item. Don't forget to leave space for breaks and food, and beware of the planning fallacy!

4. Commit to your calendar. You can do all the planning and scheduling you want, but if you aren't willing to commit to it, you aren't going to get your work done.

If you are consistently and predictably operating in a state of urgency, we need to both accommodate the nature of your work and get you out of the vicious cycle. Where to start? Block some time out, so you have space to play catch-up, breathe, react and respond. Be careful, though, to protect it for your adaptive capacity. Don't use it up as surge capacity.

If something super-urgent happens, cancel something else in your diary and use your surge capacity that way.

What if you decided your adaptive capacity time would be from 4 pm to 5.30 pm every day and you simply blocked out one and a half hours at the end of the working day to assess where you are at? You would need to compress a little earlier in the day (by defragging), but this margin or buffer would give you the space to respond appropriately to whatever was urgent.

One client I work with says that at 3 pm every day, the phone starts ringing off the hook with urgent orders that need to be delivered the next day. It's almost like clockwork! Because it is predictable, they are able to schedule around it and make sure no-one has any meetings booked or plans for any other activities after 3. Occasionally, it's not as busy as expected, which gives people a margin to catch their breath.

I know of many workplaces that have instigated a 'no meetings on Friday afternoons' rule, refunding time for thinking, catching up and having space in their otherwise back-to-back days.

I tend to keep Mondays free for unexpected stuff. I need space in my world for new clients, or when an extraordinary opportunity lands or something new and amazing happens. I know some consultants wear their busyness like a badge of honour. 'I'm booked out for six months!' they declare with pride. To be fair, I used to be like that too, until I realised I could be booked out to 85 per cent, leaving room to write books, think differently about my work, attract new clients in new markets, and still bring home the bacon. My life by design was based on the motto 'days down, dollars up'. Could I earn the same or more income, but be working fewer hours?

It's up to you what you do with your refund and what you protect it for.

Delegate

Right now you may be thinking, 'All right, I'm going to carve some time out, get my refund and have the capacity to do the important things in my life!' I congratulate you! But it's likely you are also wondering who is going to do all this other stuff that still has to be done. If you were following the time frames introduced in chapter 1, you may be thinking that getting up a little earlier in the day is the way to find your refund.

In the short term you may have the stamina to get up earlier, stay later and outwork the demands you face, but this may not be sustainable over time. There is a direct correlation to the amount of work you can achieve and each person you empower to contribute.

Jesse Sostrin, leadership expert, author and contributor to the *Harvard Business Review*, says while it may seem difficult at first, elevating your impact requires you to embrace an unavoidable leadership paradox: you need to be 'more essential and less involved'.

Being essential means making decisions and choices, strategising and planning. Being involved is doing the work. When you hold on to work or tasks, you are confusing being involved with being essential. But the two are not the same, just as being busy and being productive are not the same.

Whether you are a manager, a leader or a business owner, your ability to inspire those around you to step up will determine your future success. This is one area of my business I don't have a lot of trouble with. I am always asking myself,

'Who is the best person to do this?' In a small business, there is of course the cost involved in paying someone else to do something, but I am very aware of the cost of my trying to do something on which I'm not an expert. By sharing this load with my trusted team, I am giving myself capacity to do what I do best!

Delegation can be a bit of a dirty word for some managers because it's a skill that can be difficult to master. It requires us first to stop, take stock and decide what's important (see chapter 4), and then to define and defrag. It's not something we suddenly can do or are immediately good at; it's something we have to work up to and work on.

We have all sorts of blockers to delegation. Take a look at this list and see how many you agree with:

» I hate dumping jobs on people who are already too busy.

» People might think that I'm lazy, that I'm not doing anything.

» I'm more of a 'doer' than a delegator. I like doing these things and I'm not sure I'd have the same sense of achievement if I took on new, unfamiliar work.

» I can do this better than anyone else—I have the most experience.

» It's just a habit—I do it almost before I realise it's done.

» I don't know anyone well enough to know who could do my stuff.

» I am confident that if I do the task it will be done right.

» There's no time to delegate. I need results quickly, so it's easier to do the job myself.

» Others don't have the information I have to make the best decisions.

» I don't know how to delegate effectively and efficiently.

Often it's our need to be in control that prevents us from delegating. To determine whether you can delegate, ask yourself the following questions:

» Is it a repeat task? If so, it will save time in the long run if you teach someone else to do it.

» Would someone else better qualified or experienced do it better?

» Would it be a great way to develop someone else's skills?

» Would my time be better spent doing other things that bring greater value?

For those of you still dwelling on your reluctance to delegate, remember this. Delegation is not only about giving other people work to do; it's also a development opportunity for them.

If you don't delegate, you are either denying a team member the opportunity to learn and grow, or wasting your precious refund doing tasks that should be done by specialists, who can do them faster than you anyway!

15% TIP

Protect the mornings. If you spend your refund in the morning when your mental alertness is at its highest, you will get a better return than if you leave it until lunchtime or beyond.

Summer hours

One of my global client organisations has instigated 'summer hours', when their people can finish work at lunchtime on Fridays. It's based on research indicating that productivity goes down by 20 per cent during the summer months, with projects taking 13 per cent longer to complete as employees aren't as focused as usual and tend to be 45 per cent more distracted.

They took on board feedback from working parents about the difficulty of managing kids over school holidays, and they saw it as an attraction and retention strategy.

The benefits were many, including:

» increased productivity

» reduced absenteeism

» increased mental wellbeing (as measured by reduction in use of employee assistance programs)

» improved morale (as measured by employee engagement surveys); people cite summer hours as key to recommending the company to their friends

» reduced stress; with the option of being able to work longer hours earlier in the week, employees could take three-day weekends and benefit from nice weather

» reduced fatigue; employees can self-manage their work time and down time.

What similar rule or ritual could you put in place that could help you get your refund and spend it wisely?

CONDUCT AN EXPERIMENT

EXPERIMENT 7

I love this activity, called '5-4-3-2-1', from digital product designer Ryder Carroll's *The Bullet Journal Method*. I have adapted it slightly here. All you need is a sheet of A4 paper.

1. Holding the sheet in landscape position, fold it in half vertically.

2. Write at the top of the left half 'Professional' and at the top of the right 'Personal'. Draw a line underneath these headings.

3. Now draw lines so the remainder of the page is divided into 5 segments.

4. Number each segment, counting down from 5. These stand for:

   » 5 years: What do you want to achieve in the next five years?

   » 4 quarters: What do you want to achieve over the next year?

   » 3 months: What do you want to get done in the next quarter?

» 2 weeks: What do you need to complete in the next two weeks?

» 1 day: What must you do in the next 24 hours?

5. Make a mark next to the highest priority items in each list.

6. The idea is that you aren't allowed to move on to the next most important item until either the first one is completed or you have decided you are not going to do it.

This table gives an example.

	Personal life	Professional life
5 years	Own 3 investment properties	Promotion to partner or senior manager*
	Kids finish high school*	Doing an international assignment
	Family holiday in Europe	
4 quarters	Increase net worth by $50K	Lead a team project*
	College/university applications for Jane*	Build my network with regional and international colleagues
	Put funds into holiday account	

	Personal life	**Professional life**
3 months	Review budget and financial plan	Apply for leadership development training*
	Co-create a study and homework plan with the kids*	Volunteer to present at regional forum
	Hang a map of Europe on the wall in the family room	
2 weeks	Set up automatic payments for network and holiday accounts	Discuss leadership development training and regional forums with manager at my next 1:1*
	Book annual leave around the time that Jane's exams are happening, to support her*	
1 day	Investigate short/ medium-term investment options*	Prepare for 1:1 meeting with manager*
		Review regional forum schedule

PAUSE FOR A MOMENT

What work do you have that can be batched easily?

Can you identify at least five tasks you can delegate to others in the next two weeks?

How can you set fixed times for your tasks for greater efficiency?

Final chapter bonus!

In 2019 I published *The First 2 Hours*, which describes a framework you can use to help you defrag your day by condensing and batching work according to the required intensity (brain power) and impact (return on energy investment).

Our body clocks are designed for greater mental agility in the morning and more physical dexterity in the afternoon. This means thinking about *when* you do something is as important as thinking about *what* you do.

» **High-intensity/high-impact** tasks directly and positively affect your work and results and require a lot of attention, energy and focus. This is your most important work. An example is when you find yourself saying, 'I need to book a meeting room or work from home so I can concentrate on this.'

» *High-intensity/low-impact* tasks require you to be on your game, perhaps in the service of others. Ever had someone ask if they could pick your brain on something or bounce an idea off you? That's high intensity/low impact.

» *Low-intensity/low-impact* tasks are tasks you can almost do in your sleep because they are easy and the stakes are low. Time often flies here because you are on autopilot doing things that are repetitive or routine.

» *Low-intensity/high-impact* tasks don't require a lot of heavy lifting, brain-wise, but will have a positive impact on your world. They may concern planning, maintenance or preparation—basically, anything that will set you up for a successful next day.

Using the framework shown in figure B will have you operating automatically at a constant 85 per cent capacity, easily earning your refund. You will use your energy more efficiently and get the important work done first. Figure C (overleaf) provides a template for you to use.

If you would like more resources, go to thefirst2hours.com.au, where you can download a range of tools to help you structure your day more productively.

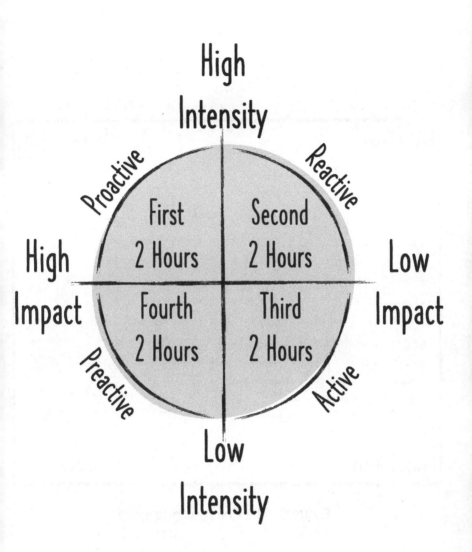

Figure B: The First 2 Hours framework

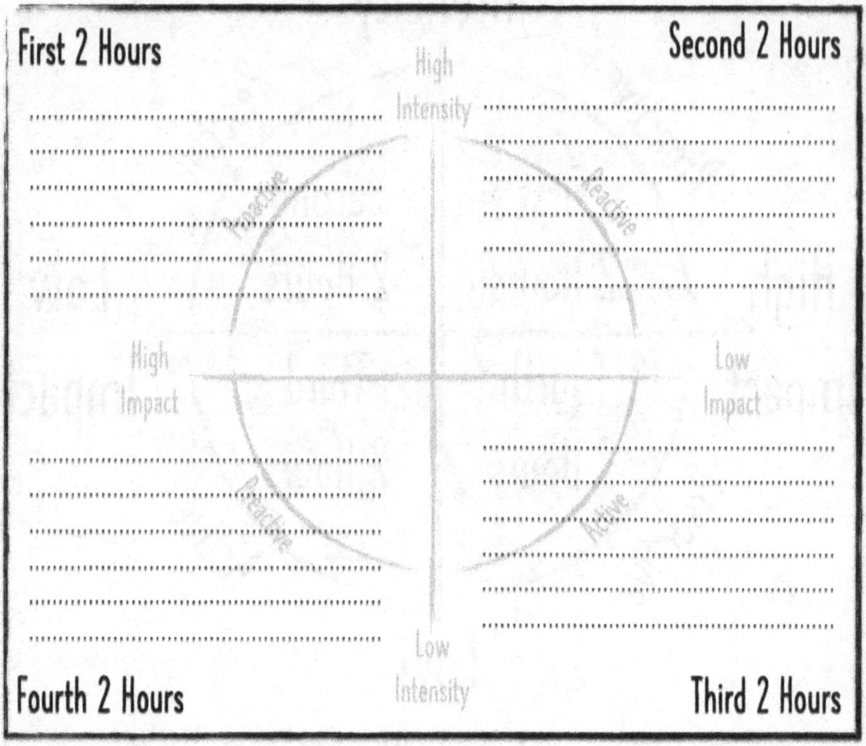

First 2 Hours

Second 2 Hours

High
Intensity

Reactive

Reactive

High
Impact

Low
Impact

Reactive

Active

Fourth 2 Hours

Low
Intensity

Third 2 Hours

Figure C: The First 2 Hours template

Your savings plan

The quick diagnostic you completed when you read the introduction to Part II will give you a starting point on which space to address first to get your refund.

If you haven't yet done the diagnostic, or are unclear about where to start, the pathway shown in figure D will give you a starting point. It's not entirely accurate to say you should do these things in order, as they are interrelated and systemic in nature.

In a nutshell, any actions you take in any of the spaces cannot *not* make a difference.

The refund created in one space will naturally begin to affect positively the other spaces. That's the magic of it!

Figure D: The 1-Day Refund Savings Plan

Where to now?

I have mentioned a couple times that in 2021 I moved from regional Victoria to South East Queensland. This involved selling our 20-acre property, making a flying visit to Queensland to look for a new home, settling the simultaneous sale-and-purchase of both properties, getting rid of all our furniture (because country-cottage style is not really a match for cruisy-coastal), packing up and driving for more than three days with our Labrador in the back seat, stopping over with parents, arriving and unpacking.

When we were first advised of our settlement date, I immediately blocked out three weeks in my diary: the week before the move; the week of the move; and the week after the move. At the time, it felt like overkill.

In the lead-up to the move, I had several calls from clients asking me to commit to work during that time, and it pained me to decline. Some were almost begging! It's both satisfying and frightening to have to tell a much-loved client that I'm not available for an *amazing* piece of work. But I stuck to my guns.

For the most part the move was uneventful. This is because I delegated it to expert removalists rather than trying to do it all myself. I also planned ahead and built in multiple refund days. Knowing we would struggle to keep an eye on her, I asked my sister to come and babysit our dog. You could say I delegated her care to my sister for move-in day.

The day we moved in we discovered our large fridge could not be hauled up the stairs without risk of damage to either walls, stairs or fridge. In the past, this may have triggered a 'Karen' event or what my family fondly refer to as a 'f#ck f#ck' dance, in which I stamp my feet and swear repeatedly through gritted teeth.

Instead, I calmly asked what needed to happen to get the fridge in. The removalists suggested taking the doors off. After a number of phone calls to the manufacturer, a couple of service calls and a return visit from the movers, the fridge is now in place in our shiny new kitchen.

This is all to say that during the move I was so grateful that my pre-move self had stuck to her guns and not accepted work, and that I had allowed for a sizeable refund. It gave me all the space I needed for a significant life change.

So what decisions can you make right now that your future self will thank you for? How can you create a refund of capacity for your future self so they will be able to handle anything unexpected that comes their way?

It's not easy making the kinds of changes I'm suggesting in this book. Saying 'no' to some things allows you to say 'yes' to others.

And don't just take my word for it. Test it out for yourself. Start small and work your way up. Here are a few examples of small ways you can create future capacity:

» Block your diary for the day after your COVID-19 shot or booster in case of side-effects.

» Get regular cancer check-ups.

» Schedule gym classes in your diary.

» Spend time researching vacation options or child camps/activities and booking them in months before the school holidays.

» Write a will and discuss end-of-life care with your parents.

Trust me. Your future self will thank you.

Work with me

Thank you for reading *The 1-Day Refund*.

My hope in writing this book was to offer you some alternative ways of thinking about how you can manage your time and be more productive.

My greatest joy would be to see your copy of this book dog-eared, marked, tagged and full of notes and highlights. And maybe a book that you keep on your work desk to remind you every day that you are designing your day and are fully in control. That you are giving yourself the best chance to be at your most productive and maximise your refund.

Don't forget to drop me a note to let me know how you're progressing.

When I'm not enjoying tea on my balcony, you will find me on camera or at the front of the training room working with managers to help them make work *work*. So if you think you or your team could use A Dose of Donna to get things moving, get in touch for a plan of action.

Thanks again

Donna
d@donnamcgeorge.com
www.donnamcgeorge.com
Facebook: www.facebook.com/makingworkwork
LinkedIn: donnamcgeorge
Twitter: @dmcgeorge

Sources

Introduction

Troy Henderson and Tom Swann (2018). 'Excessive hours and unpaid overtime', update, Centre for Future Work, Australia Institute.

Rachel Wells (2019). 'We're so addicted to being busy, Australians are becoming "rest resistant"', June, *Sydney Morning Herald*.

Chapter 1

Corporate Finance Institute, 'Capacity utilization', corporatefinanceinstitute.com.

Javier Romero (2020). 'This "85 per cent rule" will change your perception of effort and performance', 6 July, *Medium*.

'Productivity in the modern office: a matter of impact', 8 May 2013, Knowledge@Wharton blog.

Lucius Annaeus Seneca (c. AD 49). *On the Shortness of Life*, Penguin, New York (2005).

History.com editors (2021). 'Ford factory workers get 40-hour week', July, history.com/this-day-in-history.

English Standard Bible, Proverbs 20:13.

Eli Meixler (2017). 'Ticketmaster's former CEO thinks we should all "get to work" over the holidays', December, Fortune.com.

Belle B. Cooper (2017). 'The benefits of boredom for creativity, productivity, and focus', September, RescueTime blog.

Mihalyi Csikszentmihalyi (2008). *Flow: the psychology of optimal experience*, HarperCollins.

S. Sonnentag and C. Fritz (2007). 'The Recovery Experience Questionnaire: development and validation of a measure for assessing recuperation and unwinding from work', *Journal of Occupational Health Psychology*, 12(3), 204–21.

Steve Glaveski (2017). 'How to increase productivity by 500 per cent and boost innovation', January, Medium.com.

Jory MacKay (2019). 'The 4 things you need to unplug, disconnect, and fully recover from your workday', November, RescueTime blog.

Alicia Adamczyk (2018). 'Learn how to do nothing with the Dutch concept of Niksen', January, lifehacker.com.

A. Wise (2002). *Awakening the Mind: a guide to mastering the power of your brainwaves*, Penguin Putman, New York.

Julia Cameron (2017). *The Artist's Way: a spiritual path to higher creativity* (25th anniversary edition), Tarcher.

Chapter 2

Stephen Covey (1989). *The 7 Habits of Highly Effective People: personal lessons in personal change*, Free Press.

Charles Darwin (1859). *On the Origin of Species*, Cambridge University Press (2015).

Chapter 3

Tim Denning (2020). 'Why putting 100 per cent of your energy into work might actually be hurting your career', November, *Business Insider*.

D. Kahneman and A. Tversky (2013). *Thinking, Fast and Slow*, Farrar, Straus & Giroux.

B.J. Fogg (2019). *Tiny Habits: the small changes that change everything*, Mariner Books.

Hugh Jackman, interviewed by Stephen Colbert on *The Late Show*, July 2021, Hypebeast.com.

Chapter 4

Qing Li (2018). ' "Forest Bathing" is great for your health. Here's how to do it', 1 May, Time.com.

R. Bostock (2020). *Exhale: how to use breathwork to find calm, supercharge your health and perform at your best*, Penguin Life.

J. Tseng and J. Poppenk (2020). 'Brain meta-state transitions demarcate thoughts across task contexts exposing the mental noise of trait neuroticism', *Nature Communications* 11, 3480.

D. Allen (2001). *Getting Things Done: the art of stress-free productivity*, Viking. '8 powerful benefits of writing things down', 20 February 2017, productiveandfree.com blog.

Michael Moutoussis, Benjamin Garzón, Sharon Neufeld et al. (2021). 'Decision-making ability, psychopathology, and brain connectivity', *Neuron* 109(12), 2025–40.e7.

J.S. Lerner and D. Keltner (2000). 'Beyond valence: toward a model of emotion-specific influences on judgement and choice', *Cognition and Emotion* 14(4), 473–93.

Donna McGeorge (2019). *The First 2 Hours: make better use of your most valuable time*, Wiley.

R. Carroll (2018). *The Bullet Journal Method: track your past, order your present and plan your future*, 4th Estate, UK.

Chapter 5

Stephen B. Karpman (1968). 'Fairy tales and script drama analysis', *Transactional Analysis Bulletin* 26(7), 39–43.

D. Emerald (2015). *The Power of Ted* (The Empowerment Dynamic)*, Polaris Publishing (4th edition).

L. Cazaly (2021). *Argh! Too Much Information, Not Enough Brain: a practical guide to outsmarting overwhelm*, Cazaly Communications.

L. Cazaly (2019). *Ish: the problem with our pursuit for perfection and the life changing practice of good enough*, Cazaly Communications.

Stephen Covey (1989). *The 7 Habits of Highly Effective People: personal lessons in personal change*, Free Press.

Bronnie Ware (2019). *The Top Five Regrets of the Dying: a life transformed by the dearly departing*, Hay House.

A. Steptoe and J. Wardle (2005). 'Positive affect and biological function in everyday life', *Neurobiology of Aging* 26(1), Supplement, 108–12.

Clement Bellet, Jan-Emmanuel De Neve and George Ward (2019). 'Does employee happiness have an impact on productivity?', 14 October, Saïd Business School, WP 2019–13.

Martin Seligman (2011). *Authentic Happiness*, Heinemann Australia.

Emily McFarlan Miller (2019). 'How taking a break from tech for Shabbat brought new purpose to this Internet pioneer's life', September, *Washington Post*.

Chapter 6

Marie Kondo (2014). *The Life-Changing Magic of Tidying: a simple, effective way to banish clutter forever*, Vermilion.
C.A. Roster and J.R. Ferrari (2019). 'Does work stress lead to office clutter, and how? Mediating influences of emotional exhaustion and indecision', Sage Journals.

Chapter 7

Brené Brown (2018). 'Clear is kind. Unclear is unkind', October, Brené Brown blog.
Stephen Covey (1989). *The 7 Habits of Highly Effective People: personal lessons in personal change*, Free Press.
Jenna Kutcher, 'How to batch work (and save yourself hours)', podcast episode 207.
F. Cirillo (2018). *The Pomodoro Technique: the life-changing time management system*, Virgin.
Donna McGeorge (2019). *The First 2 Hours: make better use of your most valuable time*, Wiley.
Jesse Sostrin (2017). 'To be a great leader, you have to learn how to delegate well', October, *Harvard Business Review*.
R. Carroll (2018). *The Bullet Journal Method: track your past, order your present and plan your future*, 4th Estate, UK.

Index

adaptive capacity 22–23, 36
adaptive capacity
    time 117–118
Aesop, tortoise and
    hare fable 70
Allen, David, *Getting Things
    Done: The Art of Stress-
    Free Productivity* 56
alpha brainwaves 11
Angela's toilet hiding
    place 80–81
Anna creates
    boundaries 65–66
anxiety attacks 46
Argh!, Lynne Cazaly 76
The Artist's Way, 'Morning
    Pages' from (Julia
    Cameron) 14
Awakening the Mind, Anna
    Wise 11–12

balance bike (Strider) 97
batching 116–117
beta brainwaves 11
blocking time out 47–49
books, reading 37
Bostock, Richie, *Exhale* 54
boundaries, setting
    65–66, 69–70
Bradman, Sir
    Donald 108–110
brainwaves 11–12
breaks, taking 34–35, 76–77
breathing 54
breathing space
    —for capacity 40
    —in personal
        lives 66–67, 68
Brian controls his health 61
The Bullet Journal Method,
    Ryder Carroll 124–126

Cameron, Julia, 'Morning Pages' from *The Artist's Way* 14
capacity
—adaptive 22–23, 36
—surge 22
—utilisation 2
—vs focus 34
—wasted 21
—working at maximum 19–23
Carroll, Ryder, *The Bullet Journal Method* 124–126
Cazaly, Lynne, *Ish and Argh!* 76
challenger role 73
choose, freedom to 59
clutter 91–95
coach role 73
Cognition and Emotion (journal), Jennifer Lerner and Dacher Keltner 95
comfortable spaces 90
connecting 75–77
contextual markers 88
Covey, Stephen, *The 7 Habits of Highly Effective People* 19, 77, 110
creator role 73
Csikszentmihályi, Mihaly, on being in flow 10

da Vinci, Leonardo 98
De Neve, Jan-Emmanuel et al, and happy workers 79
Deborah's wakeup call 13
decelerating 49, 51–54
deciding 51, 56–60
decision fatigue 99
decision making and emotions 59
decluttering 91–95, 102
decomplicating 95–100
decompressing 51, 55–56
defining a workspace 108, 110–113
defragging 113–118
delegating 119–121
delegation, blockers to 120–121
delta brainwaves 12
designing your space 88–91
devotion 78–81
disconnecting 75–77
disengaging 67–75
Drama Triangle of Stephen Karpman 71–72

80th birthday 111
Emerald, David, Empowerment Dynamic (TED) 72–73
emotions and decision making 59

Empowerment Dynamic
(TED), David
Emerald 72–73
energy, need for 19, 21–23
energy/time matrix 20
essential, being 119
Exhale, Richie Bostock 54

fear and decision making 59
15 per cent margin,
benefit of 33
15 per cent refund, in
practice 48–49
finding things 96
The First 2 Hours
framework 129–132
5 Ws and boundaries 70
'5-4-3-2-1' activity 124–126
Flanagan, Kieran, 'second
idea' of 52
Fleming, Jeremy and Tabitha,
and Stagekings 24–25
focus vs capacity 34
Fogg, BJ, *Tiny Habits: Why
Starting Small Makes
Lasting Change Easy* 33
Ford, Henry, and the
8-hour day 7
forest bathing 53
'40 bags in 40 days' 102
free time 46–47
freedom to choose 59
fruit breaks 76–77

fuse shortness quiz 26–29
future capacity, creating 137

Geoff as victim 72–75
*Getting Things Done: The Art
of Stress-Free Productivity*,
David Allen 56
grateful, being 83

happiness 78–81
happy workers 79
hospitable spaces 90
Hubbard, Nathan,
Ticketmaster tweet 9

in flow, being, Mihaly
Csikszentmihályi 10
inputs and outputs 6–7
Inspiration and Chai (blog),
Bronnie Ware 78
involved, being 119
Ish, Lynne Cazaly 76

Jackman, Hugh, on energy
conservation 3
Jenny and the 15 per cent
refund 35–36
Jessica's short fuse 18
joy 78–81

Kahneman, Daniel and Amos
Tversky, *Thinking Fast
and Slow* 32

Kanban, using 62–63
Karpman, Stephen, Drama
   Triangle of 71–72
Kim works from home
   xi–xii, xiv

Lao Tzu 96
laziness, reframing 8–10
leadership, Jesse
   Sostrin on 119
Lerner, Jennifer and Dacher
   Keltner, on fear and
   decision making 59
Lewis, Carl, as 'master
   finisher' 31–32
list-making 56–57
lives of engagement 80
living space 40
—improving 85–87
Liz takes stock 101

McDonald's restaurants 97
markers, contextual 88
maximum capacity,
   working at 19–23
meaningful lives 80
meditation 76
'monkey brain' 52
'Morning Pages' from *The
   Artist's Way*, Julia
   Cameron 14
moving house 135–136

multitasking, evils of 116

niksen 11
not doing 58

O'Connor, Thea, on taking
   breaks xiii
*On the Shortness of
   Life*, Seneca 7
Onassis, Aristotle, carried a
   notebook 56
1-Day Refund Savings
   Plan 133–134
outputs and inputs 6–7
overcommitment 107
overload 105–106

Pareto principle 116
patience quiz 26–29
persecutor role 71
personal vision 110–113
physical space, creating
   86–87
pleasant lives 79–80
productivity, help with 58
project jumping, evils of 116
purple patches 46–51

reading books 37
relocating 135–136
rescuer role 72
Roslyn's home decisions 60

savings plan 133–134

'second idea', Kieran
   Flanagan's 52

Seligman, Martin and happy
   lives 79–80

Seneca, *On the Shortness
   of Life* 7

separate spaces 90–91

*The 7 Habits of Highly
   Effective People*, Stephen
   Covey 19, 77, 110

Sharon's working hours 5–6

shinrin-yoku 53

Shlain, Tiffany, on a
   Technology
   Shabbat 81–82

short fuse management quiz
   26–29

small things, doing 33–34

Sostrin, Jesse, on leadership 119

space, designing your 88–91

space diagnostic 42–44

space framework 41

Stagekings, survival
   strategy of 24–25

Stewart, Patrick, on
   reading books 37

stillness, valuing 51

stopping and thinking 10–12

Strider (balance bike) 97

summer hours 122–123

surge capacity 22

Tech Shabbat 81–82

theta brainwaves 12

Thinking, Fast and Slow, Amos
   Tversky and Daniel
   Hahneman 32

thinking space 40, 50

thoughts, writing down 14

tidy spaces 89–90

time
   —need for 21–23
   —trading for money 6–8

time out, blocking 47–49

time sheet, keeping 113

*Tiny Habits: Why Starting
   Small Makes Lasting
   Change Easy*,
   BJ Fogg 33

*The Top Five Regrets of the
   Dying*, Bronnie Ware 78

tortoise and hare
   fable, Aesop 70

Tversky, Amos and Daniel
   Kahneman, *Thinking
   Fast and Slow* 32

victim role 71–72

vision, personal 110–113

Ware, Bronnie, *Inspiration and
   Chai* (blog) and *The
   Top Five Regrets of the
   Dying* (book) 78

wasted capacity 21
Wise, Anna, *Awakening the
Mind* 11–12
working at maximum
capacity 18–23

working space 42
—creating 108–121
—defining 108, 110–113
workspace, decluttering 94–95
writing down thoughts 14